THE TROUBLES WITH POSTMODERNISM

As it nears the millennium European and American culture is dominated by that sense of something long dominant in the process of collapse which we call the condition of post-modernity. Stefan Morawski here attempts to unravel the complex strands which link our perception of postmodernism and postmodernity with aesthetic and human values whose roots lie deep in history. His discussion of modern art, film, literature and architecture ranges widely over the European tradition and offers an impassioned interrogation of the ways in which we understand, evaluate and use contemporary culture.

Stefan Morawski is Professor Emeritus in the Institute of Art History and Theory, Polish Academy of Sciences and Letters, Warsaw and at the University of Warsaw Philosophical Faculty. He is the author of numerous books and articles on the philosophy of art and culture.

THE TROUBLES WITH POSTMODERNISM

Stefan Morawski

*With a foreword by
Zygmunt Bauman*

London and New York

First published 1996
by Routledge
11 New Fetter Lane, London EC4P 4EE

Simultaneously published in the USA and Canada
by Routledge
29 West 35th Street, New York, NY 10001

© 1996 Stefan Morawski

The Publishers gratefully acknowledge the financial assistance of
the Central East European Publishing Project, without whose support
this project would not have been possible.

The Publishers also gratefully acknowledge the invaluable assistance
of Professor Zygmunt Bauman and Dr Keith Tester. They are also
grateful for the assistance in the early stages of Professor Chris Rojek.

Typeset in Palatino by
Ponting–Green Publishing Services, Chesham, Buckinghamshire
Printed and bound in Great Britain by
TJ Press, (Padstow) Ltd, Padstow, Cornwall

British Library Cataloguing in Publication Data
A catalogue record for this book is available from
the British Library.

Library of Congress Cataloguing in Publication Data
Morawski, Stefan.
The troubles with postmodernism / Stefan Morawski; with
a foreward by Zygmunt Bauman. – 1st ed.
p. cm.
Simultaneously published in the USA and Canada.
Includes index.
ISBN 0–415–09386–4 (hard: alk. paper)
1. Postmodernism. 2. Culture. 3. Civilization, Modern–1950–
I. Title.
B831.2.M67 1995
149–dc20 95–16085
CIP

ISBN 0–415–09386–4

CONTENTS

FOREWORD

Primum Philosophari is the title which the editors of a volume of essays, dedicated to Stefan Morawski on his 70th birthday in 1991, gave to their collection. The title is a fair reflection of Morawski's life, lived in the service of philosophy in its primal, and still the only genuine, sense: that of the love of wisdom. To that service Morawski has given his unswerving loyalty. There was never a question where Morawski's priorities lie.

The spread of testimonial essays included in the *Primum Philosophari* volume reflects the breadth of Morawski's competence, erudition and interest, much as the geographical distribution of contributors shows the scope of his influence on contemporary philosophy of culture and theory and history of art. In recognition of his unequalled role in the continuation and enrichment of their discipline, the International Committee of Aesthetics elected Morawski its Honorary President at its congress held in Madrid in 1992.

European philosophy of art has long availed itself of Morawski's thorough, meticulous and conclusive studies in contemporary art philosophy, theory and history, as well as his many inspiring syntheses; it is a matter of regret that his work is being brought to the attention of the British reader at such a late date. The readers of this volume of seminal essays will be able to judge for themselves what they have been missing. In the deafening hubbub of the always vociferous, though not always illuminating, debate on the present – genuine or putative – crisis of art and debasement of the culture of everyday life, Morawski's voice sounds loud and clear. Even if in a debate on the 'history in the making' an objective stance is hard to attain (and even if attained, hard to be proved objective). Morawski more than any other writer demonstrates what sort of knowledge one needs to amass, how deeply one needs to be rooted in the centuries-long cultural tradition, how resonant one needs to be with the artists' imagery and creation, to speak competently and with authority on the trends and prospect of present-day art. By the same token, Morawski's work sets an entirely new, heightened standard for the debate.

In the focus of these essays stands the much-eulogized about by some, and maligned by others, phenomenon of postmodernity – a controversial issue if there ever was one. Even a reader only perfunctorily acquainted with the history and the state of the controversy would know that views expressed in the debate stretch all the way from a flat denial that the concept of 'postmodernity' has any original content worthy of attention and separate scrutiny; through the presentation of postmodernity as a cancerous, yet fortunately curable, growth on the still (essentially) sound body of modernity; dismissal of postmodern culture as a mere epiphenomenon or addendum of late-capitalist, post-fordist and consumerist strategy; portrayal of postmodernity as a reactionary or neo-conservative rebellion against the insouciance of critical reason; up to the hailing of the advent of postmodernity as emancipatory even after centuries of heavy-handed oppression of which modernity was past master, or even announcing the coming of an era of unprecedented creative freedom of artistic and intellectual expression. In this spectrum of variously grounded, sometimes ungrounded, opinions Morawski's thought occupies a position entirely of its own. What situates it aside and above most other views is the astounding depth of argumentation, reaching to all areas of modern culture, from the ethics of daily life to contemporary literature, music, painting and film; and the author's full awareness and understanding of the total range of competing opinions and readiness to engage in sustained discussion of other standpoints.

Obviously, readers will pass their own judgements on the substance of Morawski's theory. It may help, though, if one approaches that theory in the light of the philosophical strategy which the author pursues, with rare consistency, through almost a half-century of his scholarly work. This strategy has been rich and ramified and resists all reduction to a simple rule, yet its organizing principle was, no doubt, concern with the well-being of the human condition, rather than the well-being of philosophy; or, rather, a deep conviction that philosophy 'makes sense' only in so far as it helps to decipher that condition and – perhaps – alert to its needs. Thus Morawski bewailed science dominated by the cult of precision, obsessed with 'clear and straightforward results', and ready to abandon in the name of that creed all concerns with truths more obscure, less legible, yet more crucial for the fate of the humans – culture creators and culture's creatures. The elegance of proof is too poor a compensation for banality and triviality of assertions and it simply would not do to pile up abstract knowledge while the crisis of culture deepens and the threats haunting the human condition roam unabated. For Morawski, any new idea and any new way of arriving at it must first pass that supreme test of its relevance to things and conditions of prime import-ance to human life. Postmodernity, and first and foremost postmodernism – its theoretical and pragmatical accompani-ment, in all its cultural, ethical and artistic aspects – are not to be exempted from that test.

Morawski is staunchly critical of postmodernist art and the characteristic stance of its practitioners and eulogists for the conformity and indifference they breed. Postmodernist art stands accused of abandoning the ambitions of modernist avant-garde, its dogged pursuit of aesthetic values, its con-science of responsibility for culture and its social impact, and the emancipatory spirit which informed the work of the avant-garde and spurred it to its highest artistic achievement. Morawski's critique of postmodernist culture is both artistic and political. That culture which proclaimed as its major principles the lofty indifference and disengagement from anything outside the artist's workshop and artistic gallery, cannot but produce mediocre and trivial art – while simultaneously reinforcing the spirit of consumerism to which it has placidly adapted. Postmodernism, so Morawski argues, is guilty of muffling human sensitivity to the tragic complexity of existence, of extinguishing human drive to transcendence and improvement, of elevating hedonistic instrumentality to the position of the highest, and virtually the sole, value.

The second line of Morawski's attack is aimed at postmodernist philosophy bent on radical anti-foundationism and inimical to all (also viable and indispensable) aspects of modern tradition. One part of modern legacy that Morawski would not allow to be rejected is the deeply felt need to unveil and grasp the totalities which underlie and give sense to the episodic and the fragmentary, and the equally deep concern with the grounding of human values and ethical principle. Morawski doubts the sincerity, and above all the feasibility, of the postmodern philosophical programme. He insists that postmodern philosophers cannot deliver on their promise; willy-nilly they 'totalize' their vision and smuggle in their own 'absolute values'. What modern philosophy used to do self-consciously and overtly, thereby opening itself to debate and critical scrutiny, postmodern philosophy does surreptitiously and in a roundabout way, thwarting the chance of self-criticism and self-correction.

Morawski's theses are consistently and densely argued throughout this book. They are not, like any thoughts of true value and originality, non-controversial; it is up to his readers to decide just how persuasive they find the argument to be. But all readers will appreciate the tremendously rich knowledge of contemporary culture, which few authors could muster, but which has been solicited by Morawski in evidence; and they will be deeply impressed by the facility with which the author moves even through the most obscure and notoriously benighted nooks and crannies of contemporary cultural creation, as well as by his profoundly felt empathy with the technical experiment and innermost cravings of contemporary art.

This book is aimed at the very heart of the ongoing cultural debate. It will open a new chapter in our joint efforts to 'make sense' of the convoluted, and still far from finished, history of modern culture.

Zygmunt Bauman

PREFACE

Let me clarify one issue which will allow readers to understand better this mega-essay, consisting of four main chapters and related commentaries to be found in the talk with Chris Rojek. This essay is a portion of a larger original study which I presented to the publishers. It covered two extensive chapters which dealt with philosophical postmodernism as well as the sociological conceptions of postmodernism and a preface providing a synopsis of my approach, premises and arguments. The main tenor of my work rested on the weighing of reasons pro and con, and equally on numerous exemplifications (analysed and interpreted) from the domain of art and philosophy. I tried my best to render modernity or modernism so that is would facilitate properly grasping its opposition to postmodernity as I understand it and acknowledging postmodernism as a new cultural mutation. When tackling modernism, and the avant-garde as its apex, I emphasized first of all the motive of contest, not of mere experimenting. Pointing to the future-bound approach I robustly noted that this formation did not neglect cherished traditional values. In any case, postmodernism solely pretends to recover the past, the archaic, the sources.

All of this is, alas, almost absent in my present text. The chapters published here have already appeared in English in journals of narrow circulation – two of them in Warsaw, one in Madrid, one in Jerusalem. They have now been shortened and elaborated. Will readers in the Anglo-Saxon world who are familiar with the problematics find my contribution worth-while? I would be happy to offer them my full study, the possible impact of which I would defend without shame. A truncated body of thought always triggers the fear that too much is missing. Why, then, did I agree to publish it in such form? Only because I was encouraged by the opinion that this 'child' of mine, trimmed according to the publisher's stand-ards, still speaks in its own voice and raises questions insuff-iciently fathomed in the English-medium intellectual discus-sions of our day.

ACKNOWLEDGEMENTS

I must express thanks to my colleagues. There have been many listeners to my lecturers on postmodernity and postmodernism at home and abroad to whom I am obliged. My warmest thanks go to Leszek Kolakowski who read my first essays, written in 1986–7, and gave a positive opinion on them, thus encouraging me to continue this study. I took advantage of several talks on my research with another Polish compatriot now resident in England – Professor Maria Bielinska-Hirszowicz. She tried to cool – if not freeze – my ardent interest in the discussions concerning the idea of postmodernism. To be sure, I was not won over by her arguments, but I had to reconsider my thoughts in the light of her kind strictures – a very healing therapy! My most sincere expressions of gratitude must go to Chris Rojek, my first and strictly speaking, confidential reader, indulgently bearing my English which had, again and again, to be improved. Separate and most profound thanks must be addressed to Zygmunt Bauman, my friend and steady correspondent, who taught me a lot about postmodernity and postmodernism. It was he who instigated the publication of this book, supported me with his critical mind, tolerated my polemics with his always original, thoughtful conceptions. Despite his many duties and own workload he generously devoted precious time and his brilliant mind to my project.

1

POLEMICAL REFLECTIONS ON POSTMODERNISM

There are at least three varieties of postmodernism: social-cultural, artistic and philosophical. It might seem to be point-less singling out the first of them since the remaining two are also cultural in character. But it is necessary to make the distinction because the latter two refer to changes in the sphere of symbolic culture while the first, which is in all probability the variety of key importance, pertains to the civilizational process taken as a whole. Three different disciplines are con-cerned with these aspects: the sociology of culture, the theory of art and philosophy itself.

The concept of postmodernism is undoubtedly fashionable. But as so often happens (especially in the humanities) to categories used as catchwords or slogans, it has come to suffer from semantic fuzziness. One cannot abstain from using the concept, but at the same time one does not know how to define it precisely. This does not belittle the importance of the set of phenomena to which it refers. The fuzziness is a symptom of spiritual tension and confusion. One senses intuitively that something long dominant is collapsing or has collapsed. How-ever, it is far from certain if these phenomena of collapse are entirely new or whether the name we use to fix it in clumsy definitions (definitions which are often at variance with one another) makes sense at all. We read again and again that postmodernism is not in the least a sequel to modernism, but merely 'a state of mind' characteristic of modernism's current incarnation. It is at least debatable whether that present in-carnation of modernism betokens its renewal.

Postmodernism in its artistic variant has had a brief but highly instructive history. It is a revealing history because during the last thirty years or so the term has been used in so many incompatible ways. This is due to the basic difficulty of the ambiguity of the oppositional concept: modernism.

There are at least four or five versions of modernism:

Modernism 1 This form is based on stylistic formulas characteristic of constructivism and functionalism. Typical are the works of Mies van der Rohe and Le Corbusier in the 1920s and 1930s. Their models of the purity of artistic activity are strikingly different from what might be called 'modernism 2'.

Modernism 2 In Central Europe and Scandinavia it is associated with *Sezession* and *Lebensphilosophie*: Gaudi rather than Loos is the exemplary figure; dramatic plays of the expressionists, not the spectacles of Schlemmer; films by Wiene, not, say, by Richter. It is apparent that there is a world of difference between the two meanings. To make matters worse one might still identify a 'modernism 3'.

Modernism 3 The form which embraces all significant avant-garde achievements from the 1890s to the 1930s.

Modernism 4 This covers the artistic movements from the theatre of the absurd and the *nouveau roman* and may be extended to embrace all new avant-garde endeavours which emerged in the middle of the 1950s (since pop art) and continued into the 1970s (i.e. conceptualism with its corollaries and sequences).

These conflicting or just mutually exclusive definitions of modernism illustrate the confusion which lies at the heart of the discussion of postmodernism. One cannot be confident of shared premises or even shared working assumptions. The more so that 'modernism 5' (*pace* Bell) seems to cover all preceding solutions under the umbrella of the secular cultural trend, alien to any eschatology and transcendence, at odds with the return to the sources, the archaic and archetypal. The matter is further aggravated by the fact that most contributors to the debate recognize that aspects of postmodernism have a long or short past (Hassan 1987). For example, the idea has been advanced that performance art, which invites people to participate in the play and at the same time invest it with a substantial content in the here and now, is characteristic of postmodernism.

For me, this interpretation of performance art is interesting but unconvincing. Its shortcomings can most convincingly be demonstrated by concentrating on Schechner's work (1982). He begins from the assumption that the whole epoch following the Second World War was one of postmodernism. The nuclear revolution accompanied by other devastations, mainly ecological in character, is supposed to bear witness to the end of the epoch of humanism, the end of the epoch of faith in the unlimited Promethean potentials of collective and individual humanity alike. This understanding of humanism as ultimately leading to the possible destruction of humankind, is an axis of modernist ideology. Hence the concept of modernism is narrowed: it is largely similar to that laid down by Weber and continued in another way by Habermas – the difference being that they were its heralds while Schechner is opposed to it, somewhat in parallel to Bell. Schechner opposes it with the planetarism (cosmism) typical of Eastern cultures and with a plea for participation in the heritage of humankind as a whole. In Schechner the restriction of the concept of modernism means the identification of postmodernism with the branch of the late avant-garde which drew its stimulation from magical and archaic heritages: from oral culture, from the traditions of Japanese and Indian theatre and from following in the footsteps of Artaud's Mexican lessons.

At the same time, the scheme proposed by Schechner describes the postmodernism orientation in such a way that it practically concerns almost the entire new avant-garde. Schechner refers to the primacy of the principle of indeterminacy (the abandonment of the logic of action and narration); to reflection on oneself (which is seen as narcissism); to the turn towards ritual and in general to the primitive sources of mind;

3

to religious (but not church-based) inspirations; to conscious-ness which does not respect linear spatio-temporal sequences but is immersed in deep experience close to the mysterious cosmic elements which Hinduism calls *maya* and *lila*. Since Schechner also stresses the fact that postmodernism is based on originality, spontaneity, collective creative work, integrated and organized approaches to the world, multi-perspectivism and multi-dimensionality, we are offered the repertory of the most interesting programmatic premises and most valuable achievements of the so-called anti-artists from the years 1955 to 1975. He draws on them when he analyses the fall of the avant-garde. He deplores the fact that formalism gained the upper hand and that soloist performances have more and more edged out the messages oriented towards planetarism and interculturalism. Schechner's inconsistencies and even outright self-contradictions show how his interpretation of modernism versus postmodernism is misleading and unreliable. He rightly sees Grotowski and Artaud, for example, as modernists because they search for a theatrical element which unites everything. However, Grotowski is also described as the postmodernist ringmaster of 'The Theatre of Sources' which reveals all-human and even supra-human communication networks. If my argu-ment is right then such intellectual exercises as Schechner's prolong the confusion over the meaning of postmodernism. They miss what is the most important thing: the spectacular rejection by postmodernism of the avant-garde heritage.

I ascribe particular importance to avant-garde tendencies. Modernism radicalized artistic attitudes. It bestowed upon them revolutionary momentum. While respecting or altogether reinforcing the autonomy of artistic values, it assigned to art the role of the transfiguration of reality. It set a premium on novelty, required constant progress in creative work, smashed stylistic uniformity and destroyed all canons except the un-ceasing revolt oriented to the future. Of course, at the root of modernism's case for the avant-garde was the ensemble of humanistic ideas shaped by the Enlightenment and Roman-ticism. But, on the other hand, it was sensitive to the ethos of transcendence and to eschatological considerations.

This depiction of the avant-garde does not remove obscurities but it clears the field of some of its conceptual fog. It enables us to see that if emphasis is placed on the anti-avant-garde and post-avant-garde nature of postmodernism we come close to the crux of the matter of what postmodernism means. One might say that postmodernism in this sense is marked by certain spectacular properties that can be referred to the entire area of artistic culture. Of course this is not to deny the ambiguity of the concept (an ambiguity caused by the immensely varied manifestations of postmodernism in the particular spheres of art – it is obviously different, say, in architecture than it is in literature). Yet I suggest that the more these ambiguities are pointed out the more fruitful is the approach to the idea of postmodernism.

But this understanding raises the question of the distinctive properties of artistic postmodernism. What are they? A preliminary list might stress:

- rejection of all emancipatory and Utopian aspirations;
- palpable, even if not declared, conformity;
- the denial of avant-garde faith in the development of art through the activity of the future-oriented elite;
- the ostentatious turn towards mass culture with its laws of the market;
- the return to figuration, narration and melody and in general to those components of the work of art that support close contact with the broadest public;
- the eclecticism, quotation of old styles of art or masterpieces in order to produce pastiches or playful juxtapositions of them;
- the use of parody – not as a method of self-ridicule or criticism, but merely in order to indicate that the world of culture abounds with used signs and any presence of authentic novelty or originality will be a mystification;
- hedonism consisting in the unpretentious pleasure of producing something which, according to the institutional rules, is still treated as a work of art and at the same time affording short-term joy and relaxation on the part of the recipient.

The objection to this argument is, of course, that the avant-garde deliberately reached for mass culture as well. It was fascinated by cabaret, music hall, spectacles and the circus. One can hardly deny this. However, this objection forgets the decisive issue that one form of art reception is not identical to another. The modernist avant-garde drew from mass culture in order to undo the sanctuary of academicism, to refresh and broaden the repertory of expression, to give the public a wholly new and different vision of the world. Underlying this was perhaps the most important consideration of all; to offer the recipient a vision of reality that would be an alternative to the received one. (Recall Shklovsk's device of strangeness, Brecht's *Verfremdungseffekt*, and Benjamin's idea of montaging citations.) But in the postmodernist perspective the process goes in the reverse direction. Mass culture does not fertilize elitist culture but brings the latter down to its own level. No distinct vision of the world is at stake. Rather one runs away from this option in so far as is possible. The creative intention is not animated by the desire to renew art; on the contrary, the wear and tear of art is bluntly stressed. Any idea of progress is suspect, any intellectual (especially theoretic) endeavour of the artist is judged to be miserably hypertrophic.

If this account holds good it will not do to limit ourselves to the field of art. To understand fully the differences between modernity and postmodernity we must leave art and aesthetics and move into the sphere of sociology and the philosophy of culture.

Weber is a crucial figure here. His disenchanted world is founded on the rejection of mythical and magical thinking and the banishment of religion to the margin of the social structure. In their stead stands scientific and philosophical reason. Gradually, under the impact of technology and pragmatic demands, these become instrumentalized. Communally internalized bonds are driven out by external bonds based on the organization of the state with its hierarchically arranged institutions. Formal rationality is embodied in growing administrative networks which become bureaucratized. Cognitive rationality finds its extension in customary and legal rationality. Instrumental-pragmatic-rationality leds credibility to the maximal exploitation of natural resources. In this system self-propelling production is a cardinal value. The principles by which the modern mentality is guided are considered to be of universal relevance. Needs are subordinated to the ethos of work; one lives not for pleasure but to multiply and accumulate material goods. In this process one consolidates the goals of one's own existence and the existence of the group of which one is a member. Higher (elitist) values are in turn set up. The professionals and intellectuals are their carriers. But thanks to the spread of education, modernism is exposed to the danger of the levelling-down of the standard of knowledge. Regional and national barriers crumble before the values of the international market. Democratic values of co-existence and the growth of wealth produce the atomization of society and the phenomenon of the Hegelian *Entzweiung* – a gap between private and public life. The growth of materialism and the increased domination of the commodity economy are followed by the painful reification of human relations. The bureaucratization of everyday life makes the social system resemble life in the barracks. The obsessive concentration on perpetual progress forgets about the zigzags and blind alleys of history. The free-floating Eros is bridled. Although Weber did not state the consequences of these apt observations, his distance from what he analysed is quite obvious. Thus, modernism must be interpreted more broadly than it was treated by him. Its soil bred counter-tendencies to all embracing Reason. Degenerating rationalism necessitated recourse to the imagination, emotions and intuition. Mytho-poietic drives expelled from the Promethean kingdom of Logos returned like a boomerang. Instrumentalized science yielded a turn towards the archaic sources of culture. Philosophy reduced to a dry metaphysical discourse had to find an opponent in philosophy pursued in an artistic manner. Religion made private since Luther, under the influence of Schleiermacher and Kierkegaard, turned to existential problems. Nature, trampled pitilessly by the juggernaut of modernist industry, was restored to its authentic dimension in poetry, art

7

and the escape from big city life. Above all, there was the defence of Eros and the endeavour to understand the 'oddities' (up till folly) proscribed by Reason.

All that Habermas (1985) describes as a remote discourse on modernism (from the Jena circle via Nietzsche and Heidegger to Bataille and Adorno) is actually a discourse *within the frames of modernism*. This discourse reveals the striving to endow humankind once again with its lost balance of spirit, to deprive rationality of its absolute value, and to free and promote the energy of what Adorno called 'another reality' (*das Andere*) and what Bataille rendered as specific para-philosophical knowledge (heterology). Thus conceived, modernism comprises both *Lebensphilosophie* and all artistic movements ranging from symbolism to surrealism as well as the neo-positivist philosophy and artistic trends which emphasize the material values of artworks, their construction, function and connection with vital needs.

Postmodernism is based on opposite assumptions. It obliterates the difference between the authority of fundamental values and their being superfluous. It brings forth a flood of signs at various levels which function both as commodities and political messages. Fast and vertiginous consumption becomes the pulse and basic object of societal life, which in turn bestows upon everyday life a spectacular quality governed by marketing and advertisements. Mass culture dominates over the high-level circulation of cultural goods, and the ethos of work is subordinated to the ethos of hedonism. Life becomes absorbed by a merry-go-round of reproduced artefacts and spectacles which must be absorbed and discharged.

Baudrillard sees this as an ob-scene world which is most fully realized in the USA and particularly in California. In *Amérique* (1986) Baudrillard describes it as a magnificent spiritual desert, an unending game in which the maximum intensity of short-lived experience is at stake. The European Utopia of prosperity, equal chances and problem-free existence is materialized there in a diabolical manner. Everything is accessible: the world is transparently unambiguous – or almost unambiguous. The shining neon lights (as in Las Vegas) combine to form a reality transferred from a fairy-tale to the social substance. Reality is devoid of deeper meaning: one has to exist greedily and nothing more. In these conditions *Carpe diem* becomes the catechism because there is no reason to long for something which might go beyond the glutton's desire to have more and more. A kind of 'end of history' thesis operates with humankind put into the most banal paradise imaginable.

For his part Bauman (1987; 1992a) claims that postmodernism culture has rid itself of all authorities, abolished all hierarchies of values and eliminated all binding codes and norms. It frees everybody from obligation to tradition, and ridicules Utopia. Everything is possible and allowed. Clashing values co-exist in a state of passive indifference; they may be freely shuffled and exchanged. Their meaning is interpreted according to context or circumstances. What Baudrillard defined as the paralysing result of excess in every domain of life is linked by Bauman with not only the tendency towards an institutional waste of goods and the incessant change of stimuli and needs, but also, above all, the lack of any teleology whatsoever. People do not think about why their existence is given to them; rather they see existence as theirs to take. Nor are there any connections among the fragments of everyday life; we find in them no dramaturgy, no culminating points that could be foreseen or attained. The chaotic and episodic nature of events, programmed only *ad hoc* without personal responsibility in an opaque, protean world, is that element from which the postmodernist mentality emerges. When it is seen in this way, history may be freely arranged as a mosaic in a kaleidoscope. A television show, or any imagined set of events, is accepted as equal to a record found in archives or chronicles. There are no criteria which can be treated as ultimate. No ideological priests are tolerated because emancipatory reflection is taken to be obvious dreaming or outright nonsense. The traditional elites are replaced by managers or experts who give up claiming to be lawgivers in any possible sense.

To Steiner (1975), with the so-called post-industrial epoch we have entered the post-cultural epoch as well because culture without an axiological order and transcendent (or Utopian) thought loses its identity. Bauman thinks otherwise: it is merely a different mutation of culture, based on the pluralism of attitudes and aspirations and the evaluation of all fixed co-ordinates without a system of reference to what would be the Alpha and Omega of individual and collective existence. It also abandons the Eurocentrism which assumes and confirms a definite code of values and especially the unquestionable superiority of elite culture. This mutation singles out from the past and present that which at a given moment can be conveniently applied in the play of sign-objects. It is not in the least disturbed by the fact that criteria are altered pragmatically from one moment to the next. On the contrary, it consciously distances itself from any strivings to universalize the meaning of criteria and procedures of conduct. This mutation rejoices in ridding itself of nostalgia after paradise lost or any paradise in the future. It is a mutation devoid of illusions about alleged progress. Thus it rejects the charms of ceaseless innovation. Its relation to tradition is purely functional; it extracts from it what is suitable under given circumstances and remoulds it arbitrarily.

Bauman emphasizes the replacement of the axiological 'Holy Trinity' of modernism (the ideals of freedom, equality and fraternity) with a new trinity based upon contingency, diversity and tolerance. He points to the fact that in consumer society arbitrariness very easily changes into the incessant confirmation of the supremacy of those who have much over those who have fewer and fewer material goods; that diversity is dazzling but often of poor quality, and if the quality is high then it is accessible to only the chosen ones. As for tolerance, this often takes the form of unbridled managerial decisions and/or total indifference to the majority of human beings manipulated by the temptations of the market which disregards the non-extinct demands of self-management and self-determination. Everyone is left to him or herself. Hence there is an acceptance of the plurality of levels and styles of life alongside the maintenance and even aggravation of an unjust society. That is why Bauman states that it is not sufficient to have a dramatic awareness of the disasters caused by modernist orientation; postmodernity should also pass judgement on itself, because the approval of automatic cultural processes combined with the domination of the free-market economy and its satellite phenomena results in highly dubious consequences that destroy the humanist ethos.

Both Baudrillard – although he rarely uses the concept under examination – and Bauman – although he sometimes speaks of it as Lyotard and Eco do, as a new form of modernity, a kind of endeavour towards self-correction – make it possible to separate clearly the new cultural mutation from modernism interpreted in a sense broader than Weber. This broader definition covers both Logos and Mythos. Furthermore, if one wants to grasp the meaning of the cultural transformations around us, especially in literature and art, one has to reverse one more aspect of Weber's model. I have in mind his thesis pertaining to the marked autonomization of the particular spheres of art, science and philosophy, religion and morality, and their corresponding social practices. Habermas referred directly to this thesis when defending the 'uncompleted' modernist project designed to resist the newest anti-art trend. I fully agree that modernism maintained and even increased the autonomy of art by stressing its autotelic properties. But it also undermined that autonomy, beginning with the manifestos of Dadaism and productivism. This second set of processes found its final effect in the emergence during the mid-1950s of the many variations of anti-art.

It was not only in this respect that anti-art had its roots in modernist soil. Why? Because it represented an elitist culture even if it coquetted the public with its plebian tendencies. In addition, it was subversive and aware of the traps attendant upon subversion (the artist without works of art in the institutional art-world) and finally because it laid bare its excessive, if not outright crazy, aspirations to emancipation. In brief, Weber's model of autonomy, correct as it was in 1905, could in no way correlate with the artistic changes following the Second World War. Postmodernism is at odds with the principle of the autonomy of high elitist art as well as with the artistic

11

praxis from 1950s up to the 1970s, which embraced the new avant-garde as a modernist sub-formation.

The fondness of Benjamin for quotations and the post-modernism frenzy of citing are two different things. The same applies to Duchamp's *Pharmacie* and *LHOOO* relative to the present-day pastiches. Duchamp quoted a poor landscape of an unknown painter and added moustaches to Gioconda's face with the aim of ridiculing the pathos of *non omnis moriar* petrified by academic practices. Postmodern artists today merely multiply valuable old things in order to convince people that nothing more can be done save a parasitic use of the treasure kept in museums and the wisdom collected in the library.

If we accept all of this, then we can more easily grasp the constitutive feature of postmodernism in its artistic version: the sense of exhaustion. Exhaustion is expressed in the stress on pastiche and parody, the collage of quotations, travesties, the idolatry of comic strips, the main strategy of satisfying the public's 'hunger for pictures', the absence of confrontative and rebel attitudes, the perverse mix of values, the collapse of the humanistic heritage, vibrant anti-elitism and an all-embracing eclecticism.

II

The links between the artistic, socio-cultural and philosophical strands of postmodernism are very complex. The interplay between them was manifold and uneven: its explosive effects became evident at the turn of the 1970s when the avant-garde contestations started to decline. Another instance of the explosion was the conflict between Habermas and Lyotard, which focused on the philosophical and socio-cultural dimensions of postmodernism. The controversy was as much over universal claims to reason, the possibility of formulating and accepting a principle of all things, as the issue of organic affinities between postmodernist *Zeitgeist* and the revival of neo-conservative ideology in the USA and Western Europe.

At this point it is worth saying a few words about the connections between philosophical and artistic postmodernism.

Lyotard in his works on Buren, Adami, Arakawa, Newman, etc. (1982–4) quoted phenomena from the sphere of the neo-avant-garde which he saw as contestation-oriented and continuing the revolutionary moves of Duchamp to whom he devoted a separate, brilliant essay (1977a). However, it is not quite clear which artists he considered to be the authentic representatives of the new cultural mode. That is why we must take into account not the examples quoted by Lyotard, but the convergence of given artistic and philosophic orientations. We still encounter claims that modernism stressed the autonomy of art and prized its autotelic values and the idea of novelty, whereas postmodernism abandoned the former and rejected the latter. But it can be easily seen when one studies empirical data that the former, if one takes the avant-garde trend to be its climax, was hardly exclusively autotelic.

Similarly, the latter exactly restated the essence of art as it turned to narration and iconicity and did not altogether renounce novelty, binding it with the ubiquitous rhythm of fashion. It is enough to mention Jeff Koons' sequence of series called *The New* (1982), *The Statuary* (1986), *Banality* (1988), up to the recent *Made in Heaven* (1991). Their objects are the gadgets and stereotypes, at the same moment highly popular and most saleable. The luxury of the new areas and the mythology of upgrading them are mixed together. What is repellent (kitsch figurines) turns into fascinating idols. Supermarket hits are displayed in the same way as commercialized sexuality that is intended to satisfy the trivial needs of the widest circles of spectators. The artist's craft is undeniable. The thirst for the current brand-fresh items smartly advertised seems to be Koons' main inspiration. He wants us to share his deliberate voyeurism. His spectacle is the debased culture, the demons and sub-demons of insubstantial desires, the bedazzlement by the shibboleths of class prejudices, glorification of money, erotic frenzy, etc. Ready-mades, endless replicas, narcissistic attachment of low culture, plagiarism (pastiche) assented to as the soundest strategy – these are Koons' repertory. Madonna and Jackson, Pink Panther, piglets and puppies, the vagina and asshole of his wife, make his seductive vocabulary

13

to which everyday new items can be added and from which (ab)used ones must be discarded. Thus professionalism, the seesaw of ever-changing simulacra approved instantaneously as 'first-rate' objects and the total emptiness of existence reduced to a media circus are Koons' trademark.

With David Salle it is another story. His voracious eclecticism – transferring of diverse elements, using various means of expression, montaging iconic quotations from the past and the present which take opposite tacks, juxtaposing clashing genres – should evoke the feeling that art nowadays is only a bag of clichés. None the less, a clever manipulation of them (the corpses of modernity) can still create something new. In this case *again* one has to acknowledge the width of the stylistic manoeuvres, but the quality of Salle's work is – perhaps deliberately – not high. Haim Steinbach's astute dexterity as a sculptor or designer of an environment is too beyond doubt. However, what is exhibited boils down to objects on shelves, the very emblem of prevailing consumerism. Ready-mades are either shown in their tautology or arranged so that their obvious character as commodities is disturbed (brand-new items among the antiques and trophies). If such fetishization of art is inevitable, if the artist has cynically to accept corrupted language (the play with the homogeneous thanks to hetero-geneous tricks) and to surrender to the slogans of present-day civilization, then the *artistry,* although resurfaced, seems to be suspect. It would be easy to continue these exemplifications – citing M. Kostabi, R. Prince or R. Longo All of them, without a sign of irony, say: 'We are just like this.'

In those works which are most characteristic of postmodern-ism, pastiches of old and recent works are admitted as a natural consequence of the rule without rules. Mike Bidlo steals from Picasso, Morandi, Pollock and others and even copies Sch-nabel's paintings. In the Boymans van Bonningen museum in Rotterdam in 1988 one could see the magnificent exhibition of works of Rob Scholte who knows perfectly well how to paint a picture in any style by drawing on or travestying great creative personalities from the far and recent past. In addition, he is endowed with a strong sense of self-reflection which enables him to present a contemporary painter as a clown or as a man-beast dressed in an elegant jacket who paints on the canvas the road from *homo sapiens* back to the ape. Another example of artistic self-knowledge is provided by Sando Chia's work *Painting* (1983) which shows a giant with an abstract picture. This figure may be read in two ways: a pitiable, primitive and padded colossus which boasts of anything, or a past giant with a Moses tablet at whom today we can sadly only sneer.

But these are the proverbial exceptions. Such self-questioning, even though shown in painting and expressed figuratively, is an echo of the significant motif in modernist consciousness which is derived from Gide's *Forgers*. They are hybrids or mixtures with the proviso that some (the most ambitious) were dominated by the avant-garde orientation so pithily rendered by Federman in his formula *plagiarism* (1981). As Oliva (1982) has shown, people paint today by making a parasitic use of museums and art gallery pieces as well as of the iconosphere of daily life. Representative art is fashionable, but tomorrow the reverse fashion may follow. Traditional values are as fragile as those of the avant-garde yesterday. One assimilates the ideas of renowned artists so as to sell quickly one's own remakes of them. Kostabi or Levine are paragons of this attitude. At the opposite end of the same spectrum would be Eco and Calvino. The latter is the very instance of most sophisticated postmodernist tendency. He uncovers the technique of writing the novel, making salient its decline and simultaneously its return to regular narration. But the narratives are heterogeneous and of many types, attracting the reader's attention, whereas the novelist's self-commentaries are refined, addressed to the connoisseur. His multi-story and many-stylistic tissues are explosive because they are anchored both in an avant-garde provenance and in postmodern eclectism. The world is 'spectral' and mendacious, we are told, and literature is only a juggler's art and craft.

There is poignancy in this situation. The artist can discover neither himself nor his immaculate predecessors because nothing has been left to discover: one simply has to survive in a spiritual vacuum. Since lasting frames of reference and hopes for a better world are dismissed as snares and delusions, one at best adopts the perverse attitude of 'joyful nihilism'. What is there left to strive for? When we compare postmodernist endeavours with hyper-realism we are struck by the evidence that the best artists representing the latter trend were 'methodologists' who analysed their artistic workshops, asked about the limits and sources of 'truth' in photography and painting and still believed in the avant-garde, of which they thought they were at the front. But all these were symptoms of an attitude which remained thoroughly confrontative and intellectually penetrating. At the same time, hyper-realism was the dawn of the degraded neo-avant-garde which preceded postmodernist incentives and qualities in the 1980s. Hyper-realism came to be dominated by those orientations and achievements which were proper to its context. They included dependence upon mass culture, ostentatious opportunism, commercialism, thriving on ubiquitous iconicity, quasi-regionalism or populism. All of this offered hyper-realism a convenient road to plain language, adjusted to commonplace and trivial tastes. Hyper-realism in its mass-scale version was already a produce of consumerist society which began to take shape before the advent of postmodernism in the general cultural sense. Pop artists and the self-reflexive hyper-realists still preserved some properties characteristic of modernism and the avant-garde approach. Their transformation to triviality came later on.

How can we best explain this problem? There is probably only one way – the way suggested earlier, namely by treating socio-cultural postmodernism as a product of mature consumerist society saturated with goods. That is why pop art was still a rebellion while second-class hyper-realism very quickly turned into an approval of cheap mass culture.

I am prompted to assume that this new situation occurred with the turn towards philosophic postmodernism although it is clear that the latter's main impulses were intrinsic – stemming from Heidegger, late Wittgenstein, Adorno, etc. Critics might object that I am wrongly blaming the metaphilosophers of the Paris school for what might be ascribed to the majority of the *Neue Wilde* and their adherents. But it is not my claim that these artists followed the works of these thinkers, nor that they found in their works the recipe for the attitude of *je m'en fiche*. But I do maintain that there is a kind of parallelism between the assumptions and conclusions of the metaphilosophers about the intellectual chaos, and the statements of the painters on the artistic disorder and, above all, their practical doings. In a world without co-ordinates, in a Babel Tower with the heterogeneity and noise of languages, discourse and projects, paintings devoid of meaning, whether technically perfect or slapdash, seem to be a reasonable response.

This is why we face uneasy problems of interpretation in such cases as the works of Anselm Kiefer. He commenced his ambiguous mythodrama long before the advent of the 'new savage' painters. Kiefer wanted, and still wants, to convey something important to the world. Some critics think that he unmasks the mainstay of Nazism because after Auschwitz one cannot and should not exist serenely. Others claim that in spite of the camouflage of accusations he is nevertheless in favour of the vitality of dark forces to which the Nazis misleadingly returned. I see him as an exorcism of the old demons still alive. Also his photo arrangements, like *Besetzungen* (repeating Hitler's salute) encourage us to re-think the evil. Another problem is illustrated by Jorg Immendorf's *Café Deutschland* cycle (1977). His painterly mannerism is undoubtedly consonant with postmodernist orientation. But the pictures from this cycle convey more than the gesture of presenting the world and satisfying the need for painting. Does it mean that artistic postmodernism leaves quite narrow, though still open, passages for contesting attitudes? I would say not and look rather for the modernist bias in Immendorf. Architecture suggests something similar. For next to the multiplications, parodies and pastiches of the old and latest styles (including avant-garde ones) we observe reference to local traditions, a departure from the rigour and asceticism of standardized structures, and moreover the ecological trend tending to consider the symbiosis of architecture with the natural environment. Again, a case which has to be treated as a modernist echo. Yet these narrowly open passages must be acknowledged as marginal. Postmodernism focuses basically upon artificial reality; it explores that which is produced by mass culture and stored in the rooms and cellars of museums, on bookshelves and in catalogues, folders and the like.

The rebellion against artistic paradigms is something other than the abandonment of all rebellion because one has nothing to strive for. Confronting conceptualism as the model of anti-art with the metaphilosophical attitude characteristic of postmodernism reveals another aspect of the difficult 'osmosis' between manifestations of postmodernism and the modernist heritage. Lyotard meant precisely this when he analysed the phenomenon of the sublime and called the artist a philosopher (Lyotard 1984a). To be sure, his analysis pertains to avant-garde attitudes and achievements, strictly speaking to their non-extinct presence in the best specimens of the new trend which reverts to the canons of art. On the other hand, it is interesting to observe that philosophical postmodernism in its mature form – as in the late Derrida, Lyotard, Deleuze and Rorty – changes into para-literary activity, which in turn can serve as a justification by those artists who want to follow the road of pastiche, eclectic pulp and the cacophony of heterogeneous elements. The comparison of avant-garde meta-art with recent metaphilosophy is thus legitimate only in so far as it indicates the paths which emerge from the same modernist strongholds even though they are directed to different goals. One has to keep in mind their common genealogical connection with poststructuralism and their close (philosophizing against philosophy) or indirect (meta-art) links with deconstructionism. In the case of the above hinted-at mixtures (the self-consciousness of art's critical situation plus the tendency to flirt with mass culture), the trends seem to converge. However, the average anti-avant-garde practice, deliberately a-theoretical, submitted to the market idols, pushes the two meta-approaches to adversary poles. Conceptualist anti-art is clearly opposed to postmodernism; on the other hand, the literary essayism which takes the death of philosophy as its subject is not alien to postmodernist art practice.

18

Modernism fed on the Utopia of making culture authentic. It valued nature so highly that it either colonized it pitilessly or sought to transform it into an Arcadian asylum. Postmodernism obliterates the demarcation lines between the authentic and non-authentic, the natural and the artificial; it pulls high cultural values down from their pedestal and simply declares nature null and void. Of course it is exactly this spectacular space of simulacra that is widely held to make the artist finally free. This is a delusion which is not shared by metaphilosophers-turned-literary essayists. At this point, notwithstanding the correspondence of the artistic and philosophic postmodernism, the difference and distance (if not break) between them is sizeable. The latter is sharply conscious of its limitations; its elemental force is a constant critical reflection and self-analysis. Thus by its very character, tools and tasks, it resembles paradoxically the avant-garde attitudes with which it is at odds. That which is a rarity on the territory of artistic postmodernism is notoriety in the field of philosophic postmodernism.

III

My fundamental reservation regarding postmodernism in the artistic sense can be formulated as follows: Is it really the case that the artists have regained their identity because no one any longer lays down the law on what their role and mission should be and nothing imposes upon them self-reflection? Does their 'fluid' state of mind and immersion in mass culture prove that they have finally gained complete sovereignty? Should the discarding of the burdensome problem of the avant-garde – its contesting ethos, anticipation and transcendence of the status quo, importing to existence a kind of fighting position against gloomy and flattened realities – mean liberation? Or should we see it as an occasion for mourning? Isn't it freedom from responsibility and when the artist feels responsible for what he does, isn't he knocking at the doors of modernism again? Of course I realize that these questions are rhetorical. However, it would be wrong to conclude that there is no axiology at all behind the postmodernist option. It betokens the value-empty state of everything which ultimately results in the victory of instrumental and technological reason. Modernism was like a road where we were dazzled by great possibilities and expected splendid Promethean triumphs. When that road proved thorny, counter-measures were sought. Today we know that the road of directed, one-sided modernism, with the fairy-tale spectacle of the Utopian light which illuminated it, led to even deeper darkness. Alas, the postmodern turn rests primarily on continuing this one-sided strategy. It follows that, if my above arguments are correct, postmodernism is rather a negative off-shoot of a modern culture which grew ill and thus already in the 1960s gave birth to the counter-culture movement. The latter is the extreme opposite pole to postmodernism, as its aim was to meliorate the social fabric, whereas the postmodern approach is embedded in utter conformism. This is not, let us add at this juncture, so much a derivative of neo-conservatism as its Siamese twin. Both are symptomatic of consumerist society in its mature state. Both are also manifestations of the endeavours to find a middle road between apocalyptic or catastrophic attitudes and Utopan-emancipatory ones, which are a reaction to civilization destroying the natural habitat and thwarting traditional cultural values.

But this brings postmodernism by necessity to the approval of the status quo. And it is significant that all meaningful analyses of the contemporary period of art and all cautious forecasts have a common element in them, namely the conclusion that production for production's sake and/or rampant consumerism require a price: spiritual and biological degeneration. Postmodernism does not seem to be able to heal us from the disasters that the train of things brings about. Under their impact a collapse of culture becomes a real menace.

APPENDIX: ON THE SUBJECT IN POSTMODERNISM

The postmodernist socio-cultural mutation amounts to the mature stage of consumerist societies with their overabundance, vertiginous plenty of constantly changing impulses, and commodification of the whole social fabric because the rule of obsolescence has become dominant. With its rejection of any firm philosophical, religious, artistic or political foundation, its lack of any major projects or stratagems, its joy in the idea of existence as wholly fluid and partaking in a carnivalistic emptiness and its absence of any sense of the tragic, postmodernism can be understood as the very bearer of hypertrophic and heterogeneous information. If this is agreed then we are permitted to reach a negative conclusion with respect to the subject in its cultural frame.

At least five chief kinds of subject can be distinguished within the framework of the modernist heritage. Let me list them in an order which is chronological rather than theoretical.

1 the modernist approach originated in the cognitive 'I' which took different forms – from the Cartesian 'Cogito ergo sum' through the Kantian transcendental powers constitutive of the human mind, to the Husserlian transcendental Ego guaranteeing insight into the essence of things.

2 Another subject emerged in the Romantic era: the priestly 'I' of the artist of philosopher.

3 In the middle of the nineteenth century we come across the third subject, namely the religion-minded 'I' with Kierkegaard on one side and Dostoyevsky on another. This subject is proclaimed to reveal the divine truth but at the same time it faces the abyss between our human lot and the Providential Realm. Cosmos-minded attitudes were never silenced in our European thought.

4 The fourth subject was launched almost in the same epoch and could be called the collective one, bearing on definite master-designs aiming at the fullest possible emancipation of humankind. The Marxist conception as well as the Bakunin-Kropotkin line of thinking should be cited as the exemplars of this standpoint.

5 Finally, we can identify the 'I' which was torn by inner doubts, the 'I' split and dramatically oriented towards any anchors which could save its existential journey through the quicksands. This subject in quest of itself started from

Baudelaire through Gide and Kafka to Beckett and Robbe-Grillet and also from Freud to the Sartrean 'pour-soi', the Heideggerian *Jemeinigkeit* or Emil Cioran's self-reflextive diagnosis.

No doubt, then, the European intellectual story was a scene of dramatic clashes between the five distinguished 'I's. It is also true that in particular cases and periods they were somewhat confluent. However, the drama of conflicts created the dominant tone. Around 1750 theodicy yielded place to history-dicy; thus the religious-minded 'I' was removed by the collective Promethean 'I'. The most important shift occurred when with Descartes the divine absolute subject became the question to be unwound in the light of the epistemological 'I' which ultimately (despite a malicious demon) provides us with the category of existence. In other words, since this break the idea of subjectivity versus the Absolute or Nothingness has haunted European thought permanently. The conflict-ridden instances can be easily multiplied – all are entangled in the search for our Home (or Harbour), all ask about the alibi justifying our shaky human condition.

What matters with regard to our deliberations here is the fact that the notion of the subject in all five versions always implied some metaphysics. Let us emphasize: it is not the answers that are decisive (as they are diverse) but the questions about the sense of Being and our existence. As Leszek Kolakowski (1988) puts it: modern thought enriched our spiritual heritage which is founded on the metaphysical horror never to be exiled. Now, it is clear that the postmodern trends downgraded all these five subjects and hence the exile of the metaphysical horror happened to be factual. The different 'I's are dismissed as deceptive and dangerous hypostases or else as myths which groundlessly identify the human Ego in this or another disguise and form, as the primary dynamic force of the world and humanity's existence.

Yet postmodernist artists pretend, maybe with good reasons, that finally they are genuinely free, being no more servants of any mission or Great Dedication. Let us confront, say, Baselitz, Schnabel, Salle with such provokers of scandal as Vautier,

22

Cavellini, Manzoni and Schwarzkogler. Their blasphemies against art as religion were a genuine challenge against the culturally jejune officialdom. Those who today occupy the top positions on the art market surrender to the ubiquitous mass media and the fetishes of the latest brand. This is, by the way, confirmed from within their own circles. When Rob Scholte shocks us with the artist as clown or ape, parodying the classical scenery or the Sovereign Creator in his atelier, his viewpoint is by no means affirmative. On the contrary, his sadness is more than obvious. The perfidious play with the glorious art of the past is the very witness of the debility of culture. It is thus inadmissible (and highly regrettable) to voice the opinion that the postmodern artist is entirely liberated. He is enslaved by his total disengagement and domestication in the consumerist 'Disneyland'. While we follow the frivolous or senseless pastiches of postmodernism we are left with the feeling of sheer emptiness. What kind of a subject is such an artist then? Isn't it self-defeating to embrace the new pre-dominating insubstantiality?

The same has to be held with regard to the deconstructivists' paradigm of the apparently beneficial cultural pluralism resting on manifold likings, preferences, options. What kind of pluralism is it? Of responsible, self-conscious subjects? No. These are merely numerical individuals without individualities. No one asks about the status of his 'I'; no one searches for the inner truth which might well be a permanent phantom but we cannot and should not abide without it. If intellectuals and artists give up their vocation of lawgiver, this entails in consequence a passive, self-annihilating creed of *carpe diem* or an aggressive rivalry simulating tolerance. The Weberian disenchantment of the magical world is thus extended to absorb the elite afraid of the mass idols and conceding to the verdict that any authority is monstrous. No codes and no norms deserve any serious attention as they cancel each other out. The spectacles of excitement, pleasant confusion and the mind-messages take over. The subject is buried in circumstantial occurrences which govern an existence that is primarily, if not exclusively, mass culture-bound.

The outstanding postmodern philosophers like Lyotard, Derrida and Rorty are, one has to agree, genuine advocates of anti-totalitarian societies. None the less, I contend that their chief fault rests upon their inconsistency. Once they advance the view that some socio-political ideas are advisable they become principled. In other words, they have to choose: either to fight for the subjects' sovereignty and elementary dignity, or leave him in ashes as useless stuff. When, for instance, Rorty (1979) voiced the conviction that hermeneutics mainly attracts him because of its praise of constant conversation which does not need any once for ever decreed integral personality, he tended towards denigration of the subject. But by the indispensable force of the philosopher's own authorship, the 'I' returns through the back door. The paradox is that the more one speaks of chance or of the *Schicksal* (Marquard), which appears in unexpected events, or of the efforts to establish an intelligible communication despite different habits of mind and language, or of the *petites histoires* which join people together, the more evident the fact that the modernist Ego irrevocably returns. When you preach the truth, even the sceptical or radically relativistic one, you get trapped in some kind of metaphysics which implies the subject in one of our five versions or a few of them in the same context. We live in a highly dramatic transitory era which I would like to para-phase, referring to the concept – coined by Blumenberg and Koselleck in relation to the historical watershed of 1750 – as *unsere kleine Unsattelzeit*. We face and experience too many antinomies and dilemmas, too much obscurity to feel ourselves well rooted. In this period of the diminished transparency as to our lot, we have most lucidly and firmly to defend the axiological grounds, if we find them strong enough. And in order to keep our cultural energy and our reason functioning we can dare to say that the prospect of omnipotent victorious postmodernism seems either weak because it works against the grain of our best cultural heritage and awakens it to fight back or, if it is strong, it will most probably be suicidal.

24

2

POSTMODERNISM, FILM
ART AND MASS CULTURE

The concept of postmodernism first developed in the domain of artistic activity. In its cradle – that is, the theory of literature and of architecture – it has already proved markedly ambiguous. Moving the concept to film art runs immense difficulties because this is largely a sphere of mass consciousness and mass culture. And the character of this sphere is very controversial. Does it mean that these works will be accessible to the broadest circles of the public? If so, then why? What criteria of 'the popular' are laid down? Does popularity mean the transmission of refined art in a form assimilable by an average reader, spectator and listener? Or should it be treated synonymously with a mass culture which entails a worse quality of art production, even if it is cleverly executed (a mass culture in which it is maintained that the worse the quality, the better the efficiency of the mass product)?

Of course, some researchers have no difficulty with the problem. Following McLuhan they work with the distinction between hot and cold media where the latter are easier to consume (McLuhan 1966). That in itself raises questions about the validity of the distinction. For example, one might take the view that mass art refers to a set of products which correspond to a definite cultural competence; by this I mean such knowledge and norms which are at the disposal of the overwhelming majority of the population. These competencies are changeable; in other words, the artists or, to put it more cautiously, the producers of mass art, must adjust themselves to the cultural competence of the broad public. This is quite different from the situation of the makers of popular art who, as it were, have to shape public taste with the conviction that they improve it by drawing inspiration and ideas from the sources belonging to the enclave of high art and its producers. There are difficulties in writing about mass culture. Does mass consciousness have any strong cohesive elements? Does its tissue involve definite myth-making (as is the case with primitive and folk art), or does it borrow mythology from elsewhere and integrate it in order to stick to some constant values? Perhaps one should settle such doubts by stating that no one of these questions is better than any other because all of them are meaningful. Mass art, it might be said, is a set of products marked by a definite scope (general accessibility) and a specific albeit rather poor quality of transmitted message which corresponds to the expectations of given receivers as well as to necessary, but not genuine, myth-making. As such if we consider film art as a branch of mass art and relate it specifically to the question of postmodernism, we need also to discuss postmodernism itself in relation to mass culture.

I

Pop culture, though a conglomerate including Westerns, musicals, science fiction, horror products and the like, is a term that may help us tease out the relationship between postmodernism, film art and mass culture. Let me discuss two examples from this sphere; first, *Superman 2* and, second, *Dynasty.* The choice is arbitrary; other examples might just as well replace mine.

Superman 2

This film was directed by Richard Lester in 1980. It has direct roots in popular comic strips of the 1930s but the most important point is that it rests on a *topos* firmly set in mythology and fable – a *topos* with a distinctly para-religious sense. Its hero is Archangel Gabriel transferred into our world. With his sword he punishes injustice and, in effect, returns good to the world. It is also a continuation of Robin Hood in the latter's role as defender of the mistreated and wronged. Thus the film represents the mysterious, supernatural elements which intervene in the place of God or in the name of Providence to restore ethical order in the Vale of Tears. The fabulist component consists of the sudden transformation of the hero into the winged aeon in flames, and in columns of icicles from which the voices of his ancestors come. The story changes into a fairy tale when he assumes the guise of a good-natured reporter from a New York daily in love with a beautiful female reporter. The fairy tale then changes into a melodrama when Superman is forced to choose between his sacred mission to help others and his love for the adored woman. Finally, the melodrama gives way to science fiction when Superman has to fight with terrorists from outer space, a fight whose result is a foregone conclusion. The film is also an opportunity for the American spectators to see that the magnificent strongman is also a patriot who visits the White House and makes vows to the President.

Everything here is crystal clear: Good and Evil have their respective spaces and their heralds. Supernatural and natural forces (divine justice and human love) are in apparent conflict, but that is a secondary motif: the fatal denouement involves the inhabitants of Earth in a final conflict, even though we all know that a happy end must be the outcome. The acting is almost mechanical; the psychology of the characters does not require anything more. Special effects are numerous and very sophisticated. The *topos* of the hero remains intact; only the circumstances under which he has to act many change. Were he to be presented at a distance with a certain element of mockery, as is the case in *Superman 3* also directed by Lester in 1983, it would somehow weaken the mythology. It is, among other devices, grounded on the analogous clash between angelic and diabolic forces, now quite frequently personalized in the motif of twins, a consistent element in classical art. Superman from 1980 naturally belongs to the family of angels.

Dynasty

This programme developed from a serial into a cyclical saga. The story repeats the classical eighteenth-century novel of manners. For example, the motifs of a well-born child found many years later is very familiar from novels of that period. But compared with the classical prototype the characters are more one sided and emblematic. Each of them is supposed to represent a virtue or a fault. This is most tangible in the comparison of the noble, restrained, incessantly harassed Crystle whom we see in tears on several occasions and Alexis, a Draconian flirt and insolent liar who wants to cheat everyone. The confrontation between Blake Carrington and Cecil Colby is similar in character. Their confrontation involves, on the one hand, the sense of responsibility for one's milieu and, on the other, absolute cynicism by using anyone to one's own advantage. As with the novels of Fielding and Smollett, in *Dynasty* the big issue is to keep on top. In the milieu of the Denver plutocracy – a milieu which imposes pitiless rules of competition and makes fair play impossible – Blake is ruthless to Mathew but not as ruthless as Cecil is to him. The principle which controls the relationship between them is nevertheless the same as in Zola's *Argent*: one must win or perish. The central motifs of the rest of the spectacle are: love, marital betrayals, envy, accidents, death for which no one is responsible and to which no importance is attached, conflicts or grudges within the family.

The significant point is that the producers avoid any reflection on the subject matter of daily existence. The fundamental value is not to pose questions but to satisfy the appetite for distraction in spectators by lively action, knots in narratives, unexpected time breaks. It is curious to watch the existence of those who are fabulously wealthy but nevertheless not in the least free from worries and torments in spite of their millions. *Dynasty* confirms the brutal truth that happiness is rarely given to human beings – even if they live in a palatial home and have their own aeroplane.

In accordance with the title of the series the focal value is the family, its consolidation and continuity. The quarrels within the family go on (Alexis–Blake, Blake–Ben, Steven–Adam, etc.), but the bonds are stronger than hate and jealousy. Adam is fiercely possessive and obsessive in the blind homage he pays to the idol of dynasty. That value is bound to another one which is equally essential: property. It dominates the all-important conversation between Blake and his lawyer, while the same idea recurs in the education given by Alexis to her children and in the violent clashes between Colby Senior and the principal hero. Thus in the differentiation of one-sided characters, consolidation of the plot and the life-like tissues of the narrative, *Dynasty* simultaneously continues and trivializes the traditions of high literature. One might also note that the plot is not devoid of strong dramatic accents such as the adventures of Claudia and Mathew or the kidnapping of little Carrington Colby, and the financial misfortunes of Blake bringing his Denver corporations to the verge of collapse. There are also the counterpoints unexpected in such a work. One of them is the homosexual love between Steven and Teddy, with its tragic end, and the other is the accusation, made by Steven after leaving prison, that the Carrington family is blinded by the golden calf and riddled with hypocrisy. These episodes are significant despite the fact that Steven's protest quickly wanes and that later signs of resistance to the rules governing in the Carrington oasis do not transgress the code of the environment.

These incidents shed light upon the moral gospel which guides the conduct of these persons who are the spokesmen of the authors of the scenario. What ethos is that? It says that property is inviolable and the family something fundamental; cordial family bonds are a priceless good; the intentional and unintentional wrongs done to its members must be compensated; evil must be recognized as factual, but it should be categorically opposed; one must have confidence in the victory of honesty and sincerity which will win over duplicity and hypocrisy; and the rules of society must be ultimately obeyed. This milieu has no place for love between persons of the same sex (which is treated as a defect of temperament, morals and manners: hence the pointed presentation of Blake's reaction to his sons's homosexual affair). None the less, Blake changes his

29

attitude towards homosexual love for two reasons: fatherly love has to prevail over his prejudices and he is – in contra-distinction to the diabolic Alexis – the prototype of the civilized plutocrat. He is sufficiently open-minded to tolerate the otherness of his beloved. The series goes even beyond the established habits and norm because Steven is given convincing arguments in his conflict with his father and the rest of the family. But, as hinted above, it can be only a semi-rebellion: one has to remember that mass culture does not tolerate any genuine contest of the status quo and the dominant rules of social conduct.

The deviation from the binding ethos makes it easier, I think, to grasp its core. Mass culture and mass consciousness in general lack ethical soil of their own. This is because they manifest the attitudes, needs and aspirations of society understood as an atomized aggregates moving from situation to situation and under the pressure of incessantly changing stimuli. In this axiological see-saw or vacuum the most secure support is to be found in the conservative ethos of Burke, Carlyle, de Toqueville, Cardinal Newman and Disraeli through to contemporary thinkers like von Hayek, Oakeshott and Kristol. Their conservative ethic is celebrated as springing from the 'soundest possible reason' and 'common sense'. Their ethical core might be formulated thus: Property is an elementary good and belongs to the natural course of things. Its owner, who has acquired it by his talent and prudence as well as by inheritance, has the right to make use of it without any limitations. He or she who attacks that principle threatens good customs and good manners, undermines the sense of measure and pushes towards coercion and revolutionary violence. Everyone of us lives in a social group; we are organically linked to it and never to the state which is an artificial organization. The closest group is the family; next the Church and its local brothers and sisters; and finally the community of which we are members. On the macro scale such a group also consists of the nation, but not of humankind which is a chimerical phantom. The institutions built on that soil should, by no means, be shaken. Intellectuals who want to transform the world in the name of untested ideals supposed to pave the way to justice should be treated with the utmost suspicion. According to the conservative ethic, it is better to trust what is called superstition than abstract reason. An ordinary person may have more wisdom owing to the truth of his or her heart, imagination and good will, and above all to his or her respect for tradition and authority, than any of the Utopian ideologists. Democracy is not based upon the sophistic imperialism of those Utopians who wish to save the whole of humankind in accordance with their ideas, nor on the voice of the people, the statistical majority which is usually fallible. It is founded upon the freedom to be oneself together with one's nearest social group under their patronage. According to those of a conservative mind, such freedom is a source of incessantly renewed moral values, responsibility for oneself and responsibility *vis-à-vis* others. The task of helping others belongs to the Church and to us all. One's faith must be quiet and resolute. Mystic inebriation of lofty ideals threatens the upheaval of the genuinely 'natural' order of things, emerging from accumulated past experiences.

This conservative ethos runs right through the plots of *Dynasty* albeit in a shallow and flattened way. One should be warned against stating the equivalence between the serious (though unconvincing) socio-philosophical thought and the texture of this saga. What is contended at this point is only that it is possible to identify an unconscious and banalized appropriation of leading conservative motifs by *Dynasty*. These similarities can be traced in the opposition between Blake, Krystle and Blake's son-in-law on one side and Cecil Colby, Ben and Alexis on the other. The former represent the conservative way of thinking and being as it ought to be, the latter its open distortion. Between these two extremes we find Fallon, and other characters, sometimes sensitive to people's needs, sometimes acquisitive and predatory.

Mass consciousness, internally split and shaped *ad hoc* without any homogeneous social base and without its own axiological foundations, adopts such an ethos because it must find props in some lasting values. It cannot appropriate the codes of the liberals (too individualistic) or the code of the socialists and anarchists (too repulsive in view of what it portends for the upheaval of the world). The conservative social order had its roots in the protest against the French Revolution, as much as the rule of philosophers and men of letters, and also against the Industrial Revolution and allegedly cynical utilitarianism. It has preserved to this day a preference for the moral values which link together elites and masses and which stress defence of the private arena before the exigencies of the market place.

It is because of this ethos that the mass audience can identify with the milieu in which Blake Carrington and the heroes of the serial exist. While capital rules socially in a multi-dimensional sense, one is still obliged to live morally within a definite code. The code does not allow one to deify money and instructs one to accepts bad luck and disasters in the sure confidence that a happy salvation will follow for the just and the upright. Alexis in *Dynasty*, blindly obedient to the family principle, passionately rapacious and vengeful, defies this order. And as a 'sinner' she confirms the integrity of accepted codes in the mind of the mass audience.

II

What of the attitude of the makers of mass culture who draw on the inspirations of high art for their models? This attitude is always marked, if not by outright piety, then at least by absolute sobriety. No frivolous play is allowed with master-pieces! One returns to them as if to the purest spring. One appropriates from them and transforms ready-made *topoi* – characters, motifs, plot-tricks, modes of narrations (always simplifying and trivializing them to some extent) and assumes – most correctly – that such art at such a level is expected and needed. This is because it can appeal to everyone. In particular, it appeals to the uninitiated recipients whose cultural competence is poor. Yet consequently the artistic value of mass production is weakened. That is why it would be wrong to see it as a field of inter-textual play; even if such play were to be broken up it would not find resonance. Furthermore, the main stress of the message is shifted to the ideological or, in other words, *Weltanschaung* value in its trivial form. How much a given recipient assimilates from the former and from the latter depends on his or her susceptibility and attitude, and also on the given work and context in which it is received. The recipient wants to be constantly stimulated and kept in a state of tension, but without a change of characters and the mode of narration with which he or she is familiar. Serious and significant innovation will be unpopular: the recipient does not want to be pitched into situations which require unintended mental effort. The panorama of plots and characters should be easily readable and quite predictable.

That is why *Dynasty* stays within its carefully prescribed limits of new plots and turns, with the occasional new characters thrown in to spice things up. There are some exceptions to the rule: the repetition of the theme of homosexuality; the psychological evolution of Fallon; and the somewhat 'magical' conversion of Adam, through his impending fatherhood, from the embodiment of evil into a loving family man. But the rest of the serial – that is, practically everything – is based on twisting complications of the basic plot and the basic characters. Incidentally, it is worth noting that, as in all fables, good must ultimately prevail because mass art is shamelessly didactic. The villains are punished or, after some kind of 'repentance', excused of their shameful deeds. It is also symptomatic that because the substance of the stories is meagre and they quickly become boring, the makers of the serial look for some astounding plot intricacies which, in fact, appear as sheer idiocy. Good examples of this are the Moldavian episode or the imprisonment of Krystle and her replacement by the double whom Blake is unable to recognize. This feature, together with spectacularly schematic poor acting (almost all the actors remind one of puppets, the gestures and utterances of which can be easily predicted), epitomizes the averagely unreflexive level of mass production. But the audience gets what it wants and deserves.

III

Before we return to the meat of our discussion, let us sum up what has been said so far. By its very nature, mass culture gives preference to the atmosphere of leisure and entertainment and at the same time it is myth-making. This mechanism of self-defence was originally directed against the sense of alienation from modern society: alienation caused by incessant toil, the tearing of ever more people from their social and economic roots. Since the 1950s conditions have changed somewhat. The relentless flood of information, the need to find one's place among too many available pleasures, the decomposition of interpersonal bonds, cultural homelessness and helplessness, have cast the individual adrift in new ways. By its very nature mass culture is composed of borrowed and often degenerated myths and hence it is vulnerable to control by managers. Its distinctive failure consists in the definite kind and level of tastes which are little differentiated despite linkage with different classes and/or strata. It requires a simple moral code which protects it from the Hobbesian state of the war of all against all.

The defence or condemnation of mass culture must be based first of all on its honest description. Such a description cannot disregard the fact that this kind of culture is secondary – high culture transformed into a common pattern. There is nothing discreditable in that; it makes possible participation in the artistic tradition by the confirmation of the latter's stereotypes. Thus, the alternative 'high production/low production' is evident. That is not to say that there is no continuum of works of art of various values. On the contrary, the closer we come to the boundary or to the point of intersection between the high and the low, those works can be assessed by precisely their distance from high works. But we should not forget that the continuum has a specific psycho-social structure. Everyone who knows how to listen to the art of singing and how to sense microdramas realizes that Aznavour's songs such as *Merci mon Dieu, Liberté, Et pourtant* and *L'amour c'est comme un jour* are by class higher than just pop hits. But, in spite of their refined mastery and not trifling sense, they do not go beyond the level of common culture.

The television serial *Colombo* and Sergio Leone's film *Once Upon A Time in the West* engage in myth-making which makes a sharp distinction between good and evil. However, despite that they are clearly different from, say, a novel by Iris Murdoch. I choose to mention her because – contrary to avant-garde fashion – she writes traditionally. Her prose values detailed description, rigorous narrative structure and the constructions of characters and plots in the patterns of her great predecessors: Austen, Brontë, Tolstoy. Yet the action of most of her novels is set in the milieu of intellectuals and artists. Her novels abound in sophisticated dialogues on the problems of existence. The tissue of her novels gives rise to unanswered questions, including tragic elements. I cannot imagine the translation of her best novels into a film serial in spite of the fact that we can find in her books many striking plots and points of departure for episodes full of suspense and tensions. Moreover, the novels of Iris Murdoch are far removed from postmodernism, but maybe they are not at the same remove from the typical products of mass culture.

This proposal provokes one to go beyond the sphere of problems discussed so far. But this is necessary in view of the myth-making nature of mass culture. Genuine, contemporary myth-making differs from original, archaic mythology above all, because it has been absorbed by philosophy, art, great ideologies (especially those which promote definite Utopias) and also by religious thought. In the best, most ambitious manifestations of those fields of spiritual production, endeavours are sometimes made to 'enchant' (*pace* Weber) the world again. Of course, enchanting the world in the archaic way is now impossible; nor is it recommendable. A perfect and changeless picture of the world can be preserved today only in the dimensions of transcendent mystery. All the same, questions found in archaic myths have not disappeared: they return in the outstanding works of, say, García Márquez.

Now mass culture is myth-making in a different way. It avails itself of degraded myths and trivializes that which is revived in great art and great philosophical or ideological conceptions. These arouse incessant unrest due to the obstinate nostalgia for an order of permanent values, for the transcendence of the sense of the world and our existence. That unrest is due to the fact that this yearning can neither be extinguished nor satisfied. It is remarkable that mass culture seeks myths in order to arrive at complete rest and to dismiss the consciousness of the emptiness or unsteadiness of being and the uncertainty of existence. The simpler the myth-making structure the easier may one delude oneself that social, ethical and religious paradigms are age-old, always the same, and that they can solve all our problems once and for ever.

For its part, postmodernism as I see and understand it is a desperate denial of all myth-making, whether genuine or degraded. It takes up old and new myths, toys with them, and destroys their seriousness. It finds the assumptions of *homo mythologicus* (an inner impulse to thinking of a definite type) not as legitimate but as a hallucinatary effort to import a stable sense on everything inside and outside us. Postmodernism is so consistently destructive that what it fears most – as the devil fears holy water – as its own mythologization. Those fears are not groundless. Even the most self-conscious postmodernists hardly avoid this trap. It is thus distinctly palpable in the works of Cindy Sherman and Julian Schnabel. They are mythographers who oscillate between distance from the surrounding stereotypes and the latter's affirmation. However they too reinforce the myth of limitless and happy consumption.

Our discussion of mass culture seems to have taken us a long way from the problem of what constitutes postmodern film art. But it was the necessary anchorage for the exploration of this problem. My own candidates for postmodern films are *Swan Song* by Robert Gliński (a strong one); *Young Frankenstein* by Mel Brooks (a moderately weak one) and *Déjà Vu* by Julius Machulski (the weakest of the three).

Swan Song

This film is a polymorphic conglomerate of gags of various dates, textures and qualities. Boleslaw Michatek, its scriptwriter, must be credited with a combination of pastiche and auto-parody which reveals double helplessness: that of the hero of the film (who is a famous film director) and that of the two film-makers. The film is concerned by, and concerns, the exhaustion not so much of inventiveness as genuine inspirations to film art. I cannot say whether or not the film-makers have risen to the occasion: the sadness of the comedy is accompanied by its lack of strength. The tune of elegy becomes the tune of powerlessness; the artist can only repeat his own ideas and those of other people and make an eclectic mixture of them. The auto-thematic motif which has a fine genealogy from Gide's *Forgers* to Fellini's *Eight and a Half* and Wajda's *All For Sale* has been intentionally trivialized and changed into a struggle with the shadows of the past. No mythology is at stake because the method of art is doomed to inevitable atrophy and thus the only way out for the artist is to amuse himself and others by his tragic farce.

During the screening of *Swan Song* I saw people laugh hysterically. Of course that is not a legitimate test; nevertheless it is fair to suppose that in accordance with its title, it is received as something rather sad. Does it appeal to the mass spectator? Certainly – but not because of the screenwriter's sophisticated message. At the same screening I overheard two teenagers saying 'He pushes himself but succeeds in nothing', which suggests that mass reception pertains to the adventures of an individual who unsuccessfully tries to get out of his predicament. It is probably a weak issue, and easily digestible at that, but when interpreted in this way it loses its quintessence. If one has to understand why it is ridiculed to end in self-mockery, then why pitch the film at a mass audience rather than an elite one? The former will only by chance respond to the idea that it fails to take art seriously and that entertainment-oriented production is the only one which is still useful.

Postmodernist art, then, has nothing to tell us except ostentatious parasitism on the received repertory of motifs and film tricks – and by taking this road it gravitates towards mass culture. But neither does it want nor is it possible to identify itself with the latter. Mass culture is treated with approval because it is openly commercial and devoid of intellectual claims and perception, while high culture is an object of irony and sarcasm. Postmodernism in film art, as in painting and the theatre, thus places itself in an interzone. It mockingly grimaces at its own cultural substratum, which it creates as a collection of museum pieces to be used in its shop, or as rubbish from the lumber-room. This grimace is combined with a coquettish and expressly perverse attitude *vis-à-vis* mass art which is good-humouredly pardoned for its naive faith in a permanent moral code.

Young Frankenstien

I have termed this a moderate example of postmodern film because it displays a much lower level of artistic self-knowledge and sophistication in the inter-textual game. The *Young Frankenstein* of Mel Brooks, like all the artistic productions of its director, is a vulgar processing of the legacy of film art. It is a parodic hybrid of horror and science fiction games. The spectator is invited to take part in the play while toying with motifs drawn from films on Frankenstien, Golem, Dracula and King Kong. This calls for some knowledge which entails at the same distancing oneself from the presented cinematic world. But the work can be also viewed as a merry experience without any reference to the well-known arsenal of films it quotes. On this reading, the parodic substratum approaches zero; even the pastiche is no more than sensed. But it is still grasped as funny because the mixture is immersed in a half-crazy atmosphere. Such a reading most probably prevails all the more because the tricks used by Brooks are of an obvious, poor quality.

There is no need to add that the message in *Young Frankenstein* is totally sterile. All that it has in common with myth-making is that it ridicules Golem, and that self-mockery is intrinsic to the film itself. On the other hand, one may grasp the difference between this work and mass culture if one compares it with Leone's *Once Upon A Time in the West* which copies precisely the classic version of the Western. In Leone's film the noble avenger, a man from nowhere with his mouth-organ, excellently acted by Charles Bronson, imports an ethical accent to the whole. *Young Frankenstein* is dominated by the tomfoolery of Marty Feldman. Nothing more is conceived by the film's maker than the provision of close to non-sense entertainment. In that respect Brooks' work really does border on mass culture (whether intentionally or not is a secondary matter) by endorsing a minimal artistic value which comes close to kitsch. Hence the mass spectator is here clearly intended as the addressee – something which is not true of a film like *Swan Song*. True, a spectator versed in film art, who knows the history of pastiches and film genres can respond to the inter-textual game, but he or she will have to state its poverty. The eclectic pulp of *Young Frankenstien* has too little wit and too much comic primitivism: all things considered, though, it has a sufficient amount of pastiche to be included in the orbit of postmodernism.

Déjà Vu

The third example is *Déjà Vu* by Machulski. It is of a different order. This film, with the superb acting of Jerzy Stuhr, is artistically so superior to the other two that it seems difficult to find a common measure for all three. Yet the measure can be seen in parody and pastiche. They are used here in a refined manner, with extraordinary inventiveness. Anyone who did not see Kuleshov's *Adventures of Mr West* and other Soviet movies from the 1920s and 1930s, and is not well acquainted with American gangster films, is incapable of responding to *Déjà Vu* as a masterpiece. This does not mean that a 'naive' spectator cannot enjoy this satirical comedy: only that he or she will fail to grasp what is most important in it – the perverse play of motifs and tricks, their polyphony, the masterly harmonization of elements which are so various that they yield merely to cacophony.

But if the film is thus interpreted, then why should its postmodernist expression be so weak? The point is that this excellent *merriment* carries a serious message. It contains a philosophical and political statement, concealed in the inter-textual game, in pastiches, paraphrases, parodistic transformations and their collage, on the abnormality of the Soviet system. That abnormality is manifested, above all, in the disfunctionality of a system which prevents the administration of any kind of justice. In *Déjà Vu* professional skills avail nought: the successor of the first gangster hero meets the same predictable fate.

The film carries us into the area of myth-making, although one is bound to observe it in view of the fact that its message weakens its postmodernist character. There is a tension between its openly expressed idea and its perverse, ludic element. It is true that Machulski does not oppose the unmasked myth with any counterweight but, as in the case of *The Orange Alternative* (the Wroclaw political happenings), the tacit appeal to common sense, directed critically at the surrealistic social order, is sufficient.

It might be objected that I ascribe to the film director something more than he wanted to say. It is possible that his intention was above all – or even solely – to amuse spectators. However, it is not the intention which counts so much as the structure of the film and its own face. I find in it reflexive laughter and a critical accord which suggest art of high order. In this case, then, the film, although it was addressed to an undoubtedly large public and embraced by it, moves from mass culture to elite culture.

Pulling together my comments on these three examples of postmodern film, it can be seen that refined and naive recipients alike may derive as much from these works as their cultural competence allows them to (in other words, they are 'double coded'). Nevertheless, I do not think that we should see in this phenomenon (once emphasized by L. Fiedler and taken up by Jencks) the specific constitutive features of postmodernism in film art. In the first place, this kind of 'double codedness' is an attribute of a considerable number of works in the sphere of film art which is, after all, distinctive from other arts by being addressed to the broad public. This has been the case from Chaplin through to the populist cinema of the 1930s to Antonioni, Kurosawa, Wajda, Forman and Fellini. One can also speak of an audience which is not quite elitist in the strictest sense of the term for more intellectually oriented films such as a Buñuel, Godard, Bergman and Zanussi.

Second, the phenomenon is not the source but the symptom.

It is the result of inter-textual mutation. The dialogue between texts and their fragments takes on various forms. The new avant-garde (along with its classical predecessors of 1910–30) used quotations to cause 'a semantic storm' by inserting texts into a text (a strategy also suggested by Benjamin who recommended aphoristic essays). The new avant-garde also resorted to reflexive comments on earlier texts and other languages (such meta-linguistic comments would then form what is termed a 'metatext'). It is my contention that the postmodernism of inter-textual games privileges a *hypotext* (see G. Genette's *Palimpsests* 1983). Such a text is referred to an initial text – a supertext – and undergoes travesties. Supertext is referred to in hypotext by allusion or ironically: it is pastiched, and parodied and transformed slightly or almost not at all. A parody in that sense cannot be mocking or nostalgic; it cannot claim anything which has any value. Only ridiculing and mimicking are permitted.

At this point it makes sense to rest on parody because it is a sort of litmus test which allows us to follow phenomena which can be classed as postmodernist. Bakhtin in the fifth chapter of his *Problems of Dostoyevsky's Poetics* (1963) wrote pointedly that parody is distinguished from stylization by the use of diphony: it borrows another person's words and at the same time stresses at least a minimal distance from them. If one borrows another person's text and hides behind it one does so in order to mask one's 'I' as the author. But generally the focus on the parodied text is shifted to indicate one's own interpretation of it – ridiculing, ironic, mocking, etc. This is so because parody means an imitation of given patterns and conventions of a certain genre or individual mannerism intended, while assimilating them, to degrade them or at least to call their value into question. The ancients believed that what in the original is treated seriously is ridiculed in the parody. The content is changed while the form is left intact.

Parody may cover a large family of amplifications and condensations of the characteristics of the initial text. The initial text undergoes decomposition in the form of a burlesque or a travesty of content and plot-sequencing or otherwise through plays with the mode and organization of the narrative. Of course, not all researchers agree with such an interpretation: some maintain the distinction between parody as an intended reorganization of a given level of the original and travesty as an elevation or a lowering of style. But from our point of view this difference of opinions is inessential. Whichever way we treat it, parody certainly differs from pastiche which does not imitate the original but works on it as *sui generis*. That is why parody belonged to high production and in the modernist era was one of the main instruments used in clashes with the axiologically distorted world. It was also one of the most important weapons in the artistic game when the mature, creative self-consciousness collided with the inflation of tricks, means of expression, genres, stylistic idioms and the like.

For example, Gombrowicz parodied nearly all inherited forms (stereotypes) and paradigms as well as his own resistance to them. This resistance necessarily took on the shape of anti-form and anti-paradigm. His masterpiece *Ferdydurke* is a parody of reality and self-parody. At the same time it provides a commentary on the drama of the human condition which oscillates between forms of artificiality while all the time striving for a 'being natural' that is practically unattainable. Gombrowicz wrote about this in his *Diary*. Moreover, he parodied the literary genres which he expounded in his *Testament*. In *Transatlantic* he did so with gentry tales; in *Pornography* with the Polish rural novel; in *Cosmos* with crime fiction; in his plays, with the works of Shakespeare; and in *Operetta* with melodrama and all political ideologies. Finally, it might be noted that he also parodied himself in both artistic achievements and way of life. These areas meshed to form a continuous multi-dimensional parody in which the sense of existence, the sense of culture and one's own artistic production are at stake. Any postmodernist would shrink from such a project and its execution.

Parody is also evident in Nabokov's novels. There is no doubt that he resorted to the conventions of 'low literature' (crime fiction, melodrama and the literature of manners) in order to discredit it. His narrative prose also parodied other genres, including the serious novel. Nabokov used parody to help readers realize the fictitious nature of literature. He declared that the artist should not bother about the sense of art and, in particular, about art's duties: he is to be a magician who invents a different world. He also noted that the artist competes with nature in the swindle of offering as an obvious truth something which never is nor can be the truth. Parody is thus an element of philosophizing on reality and a meaningful game with the received forms (genres).

Compared with the works of Gombrowicz and Nabokov, John Barth's *The Sot Weed Factor* shifts towards a specific type of travesty of the originals of which it makes use. It is a travesty which borders on an intentionally and excellently composed pastiche. As with Barth's earlier novel, *The End of the Road*, everything proves to have the same value and practically no value at all. Life seems to be meaningless. There are no sufficient reasons to believe in anything as a talisman. The novel does not and should not stimulate reflections, even on the decline of hierarchical values. It is a story in the traditional manner (quasi-realistic) about people, events and things, which freely refers to such classic models as Fielding's *Tom Jones* and Sterne's *Tristram Shandy*. But it can also be a perverse game with various versions of literary fiction within the single work, such as in *Giles Goat boy* and *Letters* in which several buffoons and fantasists believe that they really exist. Barth does not parody *belles-lettres* but guides the reader to their archives and libraries. In the process he mixes fragments of history with fiction, transforms the material for ludic purposes, combining pieces of the past with pieces of the present, and he makes fictional time collide with the topicality of advertising tricks.

In pointing to the distance between Barth's strategy as a writer and genuine parody taken seriously I do not call in question the mytho-poietic issues and complex structures to be found in his works (such as the logorhythmic 'spiral' in the story of the nymph Echo in his *Lost in the Funhouse*). Barth's production cannot be classed unambiguously as post-modernist. His writer's reflection on himself, his giving many meanings to the sense of the text, the disclosure of the dilemma-ridden nature of the message and the story-within-a-story tricks all point to his neo-avant-garde provenance. Nevertheless, as a 'fabulator' in the face of communication which annihilates itself, and in the face of an axiological vacuum which precludes the demand of parody, the artist takes his readers to the abyss of texts (written, spoken and painted) which mean everything and nothing. These texts have no equivalent in any external worldview and no ontological substratum in the turnstile of pastiches.

IV

After this useful digression, let us now revert to the problem of postmodernism in film art. Through analysis of the selection made within films from the sphere of inter-textual games, we can explain how the artistic interzone is linked with and separated from mass culture on the one hand and high culture on the other. The polyphonic heterogeneous pastiche seems to be the key determinant. In that respect postmodernism (like pop art which has never won a broad public even though it has made a revolution by appropriating and perversely exploiting current popular iconography) has originated from high art but tries to function analogously with mass culture. To the recipients of the former it finds its way by preserving the rules of the inter-textual games, and to those of the latter due to the easy folksiness of what it offers and also owing to its entertainment orientation and pure commercialism.

These ambiguities define postmodernism in every sphere of art. They are both desperate and conquistadorial. Desperate because the main impulse of production consists in the conviction that the deep sense of art is exhausted: there is a disbelief in any ideology, philosophy or religion deserving of verification and commitment. The conquistadorial perspective manifests itself in the occupation of the most advantageous position in the market-place.

These various points mean nothing unless they are considered in the context of a structural change in society. I refer to the emergence of a new cultural middle class, so vast and significant that it stimulates (can one say *generates*?), through its aspirations, orientations, and needs the phenomenon of postmodernism and in turn assimilates the phenomenon without protest. A correct answer to what constitutes the middle class would require detailed sociological analysis which is beyond the scope of the present study. One thing is clear though: one must recognize that there are problems here. Compare the phenomenon of the 'yuppies' who replaced the 'hippies' and the development of a youth culture which sets trends but lacks the economic power of maturity. These are thorny issues which should not be handled lightly.

We are probably in the country of loose guesses rather than verified hypotheses concerning the postmodern production. I am inclined to trust the results obtained by Bourdieu (1979) who emphasizes the emergence of the new and quite forceful stratum of cultural intermediaries, supported by burgeoning new institutions and managerial enterprises. Baudrillard speaks of 'informational swelling' and the predominance of simulacra which have to be swallowed hastily and for utmost pleasure's sake. Lipovetsky (1987) underlines the devastating pursuit of the urgent and instant gratifications which culminate in the *carpe diem* lifestyle bearing on the rule of obsolescence. Finkielkraut (1987) avows quite justly that we have entered the era of self-propelling ignorance and *mettisage culturel* which has nothing to do with respecting the worth of different cultural ethos but pertains to the accidental alloys of fragmentary and heterogeneous extracts from this or that heritage. It goes together with the phenomenon which Lyotard termed *dissensus* (beneficial according to his judgement) but which indeed boils down in everyday social practice to the promiscuity of ideas, beliefs, preferences, etc. Featherstone (1991), drawing on Bourdieu and Bauman, points to the decay of traditional economic elites, maintaining that they are replaced by efficient and well-educated cultural managers and the overwhelming variety of lifestyles. He concludes that we now enjoy a process of the vernacular aestheticization of ethos. This statement seems to me mistaken. Featherstone see *theatrum fori* today as a continuation of ancient fairs, festivals and carnivals. However, he forgets that the historico-cultural contexts change the substance of the juxtaposed phenomena. What we experience today is rather the hedonization of ethos whereas the genuine aesthetic values become by their trivialization and ubiquity annihilated (*pace* Baudrillard, especially in *La Transparence du Mal*).

V

The examples of film which I have quoted could, of course, be extended. Before I add to the list I shall try to reject those which are cited by film and television critics in a way that I think is misleading. One can fully agree that David Lynch's *Blue Velvet* (1986) has as its subject some motives typical of the present-day mass consciousness on which postmodernism feeds. Nevertheless, the sado-masochism and atmosphere of fear bordering on lunacy in which the hero is embroiled by Dorothy does not qualify it unequivocally as a postmodernist message. There is too much here of mass culture and not enough of playing with it. Woody Allen's *Zelig* (1983) parodies definite *topoi* in American life – the need for psychoanalytic illumination, noisy advertising intended to publicize success, extravagance which pays. It also employs quasi-archival footage and documentary fragments mixed with interviews of persons who are on friendly terms with the famous Leonard. Yet in practice all of this serves the main subject which is 'the chameleon syndrome' plus the blind belief that what is fashionable is best. Allen, it might be said, distances himself from these phenomena which precisely form the themes of everyday life and are exploited with applause by postmodernism. Citing his *Bananas* with the remake of the episode from the Odessa Steps does not hit the mark: the fragment bears no relation to the rest of the film. It is the provocative joke of the New York intellectual who on other occasions ridicules and parodies himself by referring to the tradition of 'Jewish wisdom'.

It is different in the case of *Raiders of the Lost Ark* (1980) by Spielberg, which is full of pastiche-like references to the work of Lucas, science fiction and Spielberg himself. Next to the excellent craftmanship for the mass spectator we sense in the film an attitude also encountered in *Déjà Vu*: transcending the mere joy which the masterly command of the workshop provides in order to convey a serious message – in this case, some secret forces of nature worth being treated as taboo.

However, more to the point are Polanski's *Frantic* (1988) and Lester's *Superman 3* (1983). Lester pastiches himself in the film by introducing the hero in the same profile interpreted by the same actor and involved in similar adventures. But the pastiche changes into a parody because the noble Superman under the influence of the evil demon (this time a product of a computer) instead of saving oppressed humankind gets into more trouble, suffers an utter defeat and after that becomes a hopeless alcoholic. It is true that the computer programmer forms an alliance with the desperate hero and that finally good prevails over evil, but the simple and unambiguous ethos specific to mass culture is here considerably impaired. *Frantic* is a fantastic, ambiguous work. Its ambiguity is not a result of its being a pastiche made of various fragments drawn from different contexts; it is global in character and draws on American crime series from the 1950s and reinvents the aura of Alfred Hitchcock's films. Moreover, it is so well made, with such artistic virtuosity, that one cannot help responding to its exquisite aesthetic values. Thus in this case the idea of 'double coding' is satisfied.

For those in search of pure postmodernist cinema the best reference is probably to Zemeckiss' *Who Framed Roger Rabbit?* – that successful and unexpected combination of animated cartoon and crime fiction. There is not a single scene, not a single character, which cannot be referred to ready-made models. Everything is an imitation carried out with bravura and swing. Every element is slightly exaggerated to indicate that things which are perfectly well known (one might say that they are even folksy) are mimicked. But at the same time there is no trace of ironic distance. This ludic animated cartoon for adults appeals to every spectator but the bar is placed above the average of mass culture. If there is something ironic here, it consists in the collage of heterogeneous elements. The mass culture does not tolerate such games. Another instance of the same kind could be the works of Brian de Palma, who borrows from Antonioni, Hitchcock and, perversely, from himself. His breathtaking, brilliant craftsmanship is in tune with the wider audience but his quotations demand a fluency in the story of film.

Have postmodernist film works enriched art? Is it admissible to claim that a new mutation of film has occurred? My answer to the second question is in the affirmative. A pastiche-like collage of a heterogeneous nature, combinations of kitsch with parody and a perverse imitation of stereotypical games are new phenomena. In this context it is worth recalling Henry Koster's *The Inspector General* (1949). It is merely a pseudo-pastiche with echoes of the Viennese operetta and Chaplinade (the scene during the first feast when the hungry hero devours everything from all plates with vertiginous speed). In fact this film is but a jocular modification of Gogol's principal masterpiece, a transformation into a farcical musical with a Khliestiakov who does not in the least resemble the prototype and also it has a tearful happy ending.

As far as the first question is concerned, the reply must hinge on personal axiology. My understanding of 'being enriched' corresponds to other values than those which are usually emphasized by postmodernists. I admire Woody Allen as much as the refined work of Greenaway, who carries on his games with the debunking of art and the decomposition of the human body; but both are at the extreme end of the post-modernist spectrum. Both are rarities. Thus on the whole my judgement of this type of film is rather negative. I am clearly conscious that my viewpoint is not shared by many critics and researchers of the contemporary scene. According to my criteria, that new mutation does not favour the authentic flourishing of art; it can lead culture, I would argue, to bankruptcy under the illusion that it is fully-fledged liberation. Let me stress that I am not against mass art. I share the view of Eco (see his *Il superuomo di massa*, 1978) that this kind of production meets the needs and yearnings of most people. What I am against is turning mass art – based on ease in every respect, on being unproblematic – into the paragon of culture.

3

THE POSTMODERN DILEMMAS OF AESTHETICS

Since the beginning of our century, inquiry about the condition of aesthetics has been a habitual affair. The question has been connected with understanding of the status of philosophy as well as art. It has ultimately demanded consideration of the issues about what being human means in given cultural frames. Not so long ago the reflections of many scholars and art critics turned to the possible extinction of aesthetics. Now, when their thoughts turn to what is vaguely and clumsily called 'postmodernism', one asks, hesitantly, whether any new aesthetics corresponding to this phenomenon can be discerned.

By 'aesthetics' I have in mind a special autonomous discipline, the subject matter of which is the work of art; its experience, its value and the criteria of its description and analysis. I want to deal with two main kinds of postmodernist aesthetics and a third kind which can be located between them. First, I want to look at the ideas of Lyotard and Welsch, writers arguing for a postmodernism which is clearly connected with the avant-garde tradition. The second kind of postmodernist aesthetics I associate with the works of Jencks and Oliva: these authors treat postmodern aesthetics as essentially new and opposed to the avant-garde heritage. The third, middle approach is represented by Eco's conception of what postmodernist aesthetics should be. In what follows I will juxtapose the three approaches and at the end pursue two important questions: What was modern aesthetics for?; and: to what degree do the postmodernist attempts have anything to do with aesthetics?

I

The basic content of Jean François Lyotard's writings on contemporary art did not change in the 1970s when he published *Les dispositifs pulsionnels* (1973b) and *Les transformateurs Duchamp* (1977a). However, his vocabulary altered radically. By the end of the decade he employed the blanket term 'postmodernism' to contemporary provocative art. He identified this kind of art as a constant game, breaking down the ground rules and inventing new ones depending on given circumstances. He identified it as an art at odds with any attempt at building theories and paradigms. The artist, deprived of old certainties about how to go on, rests chiefly on his or her experimenting power and *ad hoc* insights. His or her aim is novelty but it is never theorized. As Lyotard contends in his *Peregrinations* (1988), theories quarrel as much with thinking which is and should remain 'cloudy'. The effect is to turn aesthetics – unless it is merely the practical groping for a solution to the here-and-now which in no way claims to be canonical – into a nightmare.

In 1979, when he deliberated on the philosophy of painting, Lyotard confronted the aesthetic discourse directly. His frame of reference was the relationship between Diderot and Vernet. He explored their exchangeable roles and the convertibility of the artist and the critic who teach each other how to theorize about art. Lyotard suggests that today, when the old cherished values are shaky or dethroned, the roles overlap and no definite system of thought (especially with respect to art which is obsessed with the playful alteration of rules) is acceptable. The artist and the philosopher move on the same quicksands where they circumstantially command polymorphic, untidy, aleatory and heterogeneous elements. What, then, remains of aesthetics? Shall it speak the language of art or the language of philosophy – or both simultaneously? What seems to remain is particular ephemeral criticism answering to the instantaneously displayed rules. What seems then to follow is aesthetics committing suicide.

In the 1980s Lyotard turned to the category of the sublime

(see *Les immateriaux*, 1984c). Consciously drawing upon Kant's conception of the sublime, Lyotard nevertheless interpreted it in his own specific way. The Kantian teleology of wedding the aesthetic to the ethical is neglected – a neglect which goes perfectly with Lyotard's assumption that the particular realms of thought and discourse are incommensurable. Lyotard's idea of sublimity as 'no-form' (*l'informe*) stems from the artist's powers of invention, his inventive game with signs and discourses (which, of course, is not foreseeable), his insatiable pursuit of dissent or rather strife expressed in permanent instability and uncertainty. In the split and fragmented reality with no room for the artistic 'I', the misty sublime replaces relatively ordered structures.

In the year 1989 in a conversation with Christine Pries (published one year later) Lyotard talked – drawing in a roundabout way on the Kantian dowry – of an obscure aesthetic ontology which makes us ethically sensitive and responsible because of our guilty conscience. This conscience is close to the feeling of sublime, filled up with both melancholy and enthusiasm. The question of ethos was left unsolved. Anyhow, the Kantian motive serves Lyotard's argument that the experience of the sublime is one of the chief barriers against any theorizing (not to speak of the systematic structuring of concepts). This marks again one of the main differences between Kant and Lyotard. As much as the former laid emphasis on nature transcendentally grasped in the sublime, with Lyotard it is culture (and art) that should be grasped. The idea of the sublime is rooted in the unknown, the black hole of Being, the immaterial. Lyotard infers from this that any union of artistic practice with new technological and information control, just as much as any co-operation with the requirements of the market, would kill the sublime. One cannot imagine a more peremptory and clear declaration of the avant-garde *credo*.

In Lyotard's *Peregrinations* we learn that philosophizing on art and aesthetic experience is inevitable, but aesthetics is superfluous. According to Lyotard's interpretation of Kant no cognitive synthesis, no transcendental subject is needed to do justice to the particular artistic occurrences and imaginative-affective responses grounded in sensuality. For this kind of synthesis becomes impossible when we pass to the sublime. Lyotard tried to demonstrate how the trend towards minimal art, *arte povera*, immaterial art developed out of the stubborn but vain attempts to embody the unpresentable. For Lyotard the same great and fascinating dilemma was rehearsed by Duchamp.

Can one therefore suggest that aesthetics corresponds precisely to the unfathomable sublime and the uncertainty of facing the heterogeneity of artworks? Lyotard would say no. Aesthetics must be altogether dismissed when the only rule is the see-saw of rules. Let us remember that, after the late 1970s, when referring to the sublime, Lyotard has in mind chiefly avant-garde praxis (that is, the followers of Duchamp in their various shades). What was named anti-art is according to him another art underscored by a constant experimentation against fixed principles.

Moreover, what seems at first sight paradoxical – the subordination of the newest avant-garde transgression to the postmodernist strategy – ceases to startle when we remind ourselves of Lyotard's position since the beginning of the 1980s. Then he made it clear that the prefix 'post' refers only to a new mental situation *within the boundaries of modernism* (Lyotard 1985, Ch 1). With reference to Benjamin and Adorno, Lyotard argues that the supremacy of techno-science under the umbrella of present-day capitalism destroys the spirit of avant-garde which is, he says, closely associated with the sublime (the idea that cannot be presentable). However, the modernist sublime is melancholic and nostalgic after the good form, appropriate taste, beauty, or even something absolute that was evidenced by Proust, the expressionists, de Chirico, Malevich and the like. Instead the postmodernist sublimity (as in Joyce, Lissitski or Duchamp) is radically cleansed of the above melancholy and nostalgia and opposed to looking for unity and consensus. What it is after is constant experiment (*novatio*). This is a dubious distinction and not quite a convincing interpretation of quoted artists but let us accept it in order to understand Lyotard's arguments more clearly.

For him, then, postmodernity is but a modus of modernity, a paradoxical *future anterieur*. Thus to become a genuine modernist avant-gardist one must first be a postmodernist (i.e. break the given rules and all theory fixing them). Aesthetics is only an impediment in the perspective of such an enterprise. One wonders for what purpose Lyotard needs the concept of postmodernism if it consists in intransigent avant-garde endeavours. Lyotard thinks that what remains of aesthetics is at most a para-aesthetics accompanying the practice of artist-philosopher (or vice versa). This is only a poor shadow of aesthetics, since it does not lament the total loss of paradigms, nor even of flexible criteria of valuations.

Perhaps aesthetics should turn into a deconstructive analysis of its own entire heritage. Perhaps it should ask which mistakes it nurtured and cherished as gospel truth. Such solutions would be adequate in the light of what Lyotard thinks of the philosophical tradition and his understanding of philosophy as beheading the phantoms and illusions drawn from the firm and blind belief in universal ways and principles unifying the contingent multiplicity. Certainly, Lyotard's approach to the problem of aesthetics, his favourite examples, through which he shows why *un-form* opens new artistic horizons (Butor, Newman, Adami, Buren) leave no doubt that what is at stake is the meaning of the endeavours of the newest avant-garde.

Wolfgang Welsch provides a somewhat different case. In his *Aesthetisches Denken* (1990) he bids farewell to modern aesthetics. The reason is that modern aesthetics is unable to fit into the cultural demands of our time which blur or simply efface the distinction between the real and the fictitious. For Welsch, the whole tradition of aesthetic discourse since Baumgarten has to be revised. He maintains that a genuine *aisthesis* – not merely as the sensuous embodiment of ideas conflated with feeling but as the capacity to render the peculiar logic or un-logic of the inner and outer worlds – lies at the foundation of philosophic thinking. Instead of looking for autotelic values of art and an autonomous aesthetic experience, we should concentrate on *Sinnwahrnehmung*, that is, rendering the meaning of who we are and of the world around us as a total flow of unbroken, intersected pieces and as a bundle of masks, appearances and events.

Welsch's contention is that Logos stands for one type of rationality. However, there are many kinds of rationality which are synthesized by what he calls 'the transversal reason' nourished by imaginative reflection and responsive to the divergences of reality, its heterogeneous and fractured juxtapositions of changing elements. Art is the most sensitive instrument for this reflection and response. As such, aesthetic thinking becomes, in effect, the matrix of the most accurate philosophizing. In the Introduction to *Aesthetik im Widerstreit* (1990), Welsch announces that the rise of the aesthetic (i.e. its arresting preponderance) in philosophy marks the general postmodern-modern watershed after three preceding stages characteristic of modernity, namely the subsequent domination of ontological, epistemological and linguistic perspectives.

Why the aesthetico-philosophical break? First, because we became conscious that reality is constructed instead of given. Second, because of the plurality of discourses and criteria of interpretation (valuation) – its model is art starting with its twentieth-century transformations. Third, because the fictitious reality is built of open, flexible structures, the best examples of which are the avant-garde works. Finally, because the contemporary world is dominated by media and technology to which art responded through the defence of *aisthesis* versus the techno-media domination or the surrender which results inevitably in *an-aisthesis*.

Against Welsch's conclusions one could plausibly argue that what he proposes is non-aesthetics because he not only avoids dealing with the aesthetic realm but also rejects the extension of artistic-aesthetic categories to the extra-artistic world. His attitude towards anti-art and anti-aesthetics is equally negative. The opposition to *aisthesis*, he concludes, is the anaesthetic reality relayed and orchestrated by the ubiquitous, commercialized mass media. But how does this claim fit into his thesis of the aestheticization of present-day culture? Such an aesthetics, we read, has to be done away with, but why, if it marks the postmodernist culture which is acknowledged as beneficial?

If I follow accurately his essays from 1991–2 on *Aesthetik* and *Aesthetisierungsprozesse*, Welsch opts for another aesthetics replacing the traditional one. He proposes continuing the Nietzschean line against the Baumgarten-Kantian. But this changes the concept of aesthetics so radically that it no longer deserves the name. What he praises as a new lifestyle, harboured in paraaesthetic attitudes and extended aesthetic sensibility, remains ambiguous while at the same time he attacks the general fashionable tendency towards *Verhbschüng* (beautifying) mass culture triviality. Anyway his meta-discourse is not so much, as he claims, aestheticized philosophy but simply philosophizing on art as the prime mover of right thinking about the world. Moreover, like Lyotard he draws all his examples from the recent avant-garde. Duchamp is the central figure and Dubuffet is mentioned as one of the most forceful originators of postmodernism.

Lyotard and Welsch, notwithstanding the crucial differences between them, both find the source of the crisis of inherited aesthetics in the invalid philosophizing on art. Yet how Welsch can ignore anti-aesthetics, while at the same time baptizing the late avant-garde rebellion as postmodernism, remains a conundrum. One feels that he was, maybe, stimulated by Marquard's work (Marquard 1989) but that he reshuffled it. Marquard assumes that aesthetics has a compensatory function: it compensates for the lures of philosophy which ventured to rescue the sense of being. This is especially so in times of modernity where questions of being are so embattled. After the decline of theodicy and metaphysics, it addressed sciences and the historical process based on evolutionary and emancipatory projects as the strongholds of the meaningful worldview. But these projects were in vain. Note that Marquard does not say that aesthetics replaces philosophy and that *aisthesis* becomes the latter's main axiom. On the contrary, philosophizing on the perplexing reality devoid of any principles cannot be exiled from human thought; it cannot be pensioned-off for ever. Marquard maintains that aesthetics (and art as its favourite

field of study) preserves its relatively self-sufficient significance. That is why he calls himself a 'traditional modernist'.

However, Welsch understands aesthetics as the sensorium
of philosophy and art, and thus deprives them of their identity.
Their blend is meant to be one of the trademarks of the
illuminating theoretical multi-discourse which corresponds
most lucidly (via paradoxes and paralogisms) to the incongruity
of the surrounding 'reality'. Such a position is analogous to
Derrida's idea in *Parages* (1986). There he used the example of
Blanchot's *Récit*, which with premeditation blurs the borderlines between literature and philosophy, leaving no room for
any sensible aesthetics. Both literature and philosophy are
fictions stimulating thought over what is reality. There are no
competences capable of outlining the classification of aesthetic
theory on the one side and art on the other. Derrida speaks of
constant wandering near the waterfront which remains always
misty and he states that our thoughts when philosophizing on
or within literature are born in *paysage sans pays, espace sans
territoires*. Deleuze's case is not different. Schizo-analysis
mocks any systematic exposition of theses and ridicules any
methodological consistency. Aesthetics, he stresses (Deleuze
1991), is an equivocal term of no use. Art requires no explaining
and, being unpredictable, it cancels any aesthetic theory.

I pointed to the differences between Lyotard's and Welsch's
approaches. But what matters here are the affinities. Both apply
a similar strategy of thinking which is clearly opposed to Oliva
and Jencks. Lyotard attacked them directly as proposing the
submission of art to bare commercialism. Welsch did it indirectly by denouncing *an-aisthesis*.

II

Jencks and Oliva tell another story. Reconstructing or rather
constructing a pattern out of their various contributions makes
it possible to identify clear themes. The new aesthetics is
primarily opposed to the avant-garde heritage, to the tradition
of the new. No endeavour to do justice to the world, save it or
even meliorate it via art or by the activities of the artist 'without

art' is trusted. Emancipatory and Utopian tendencies are equally ridiculed. Similarly, the idea that the artists and other members of the intellectual elite have a special mission to accomplish is given short shrift. What is spectacularly scorned is the fake supremacy of artistic self-reflective thinking over artistic practice. Artists have to produce their works in the given *techne*. Their products are just part of the commodity world answering the public's unsophisticated expectations. The return to pictures, to narration, harmony, melody, etc. is accompanied with the feeling that social reality is built of simulacra which undermine the division between the artistic fictions and something that supposedly should be its ontological counterpart. The sense of art becomes reduced to sheer virtuosity or else to expressing oneself without aesthetic rigour. The creative process is to pander to popular culture.

However, the gratification of the audience's elementary needs is solely one of the manoeuvres. Another, and most certainly the prior one, is the perverse play with mass myths and banalities and with the expressions of high culture. The more eclectic heterogeneity, the more interesting the outcomes. Bridging the gap between low and high art does not simply mean addressing oneself to readers or onlookers of a different level of aesthetic competence. Rather, it entails treating the artwork as a piece of fashion which sells. Furthermore, it means using random elements to fuse them in an *ad hoc* manner, thus bearing witness to the joyful diversity and contingency of the world around. Hence any novelty which can be tolerated rests paradoxically on constant remakes and replicas. The genuine historical insight yields to the parasitic exploitation of the old canons mixed up in a patchwork. The privileged device is pastiche or parody cleared of any serious goal becoming an end in itself.

Postmodernist aesthetics of this kind, founded on the deliberate amnesia of enduring values, corresponds fully to the average artistic practice of today. This practice is devoid of any aspiration to carve the human psyche. It is manifestly passive. It takes the world for what it is under present circumstances –

a chaotic richness of carnival impulses changing from day to day, without oases which might permit master narratives to take root. To be sure, postmodern art remains art-like primarily because of its techno-professional components. Its celebration of contemporaneity seems to be wholly superficial. This is because such art mirrors the extinction of any axiological hierarchy which kept the distinguished culture alive: no critical distance, no questioning, full conformism with status quo; at best, bearing witness to the trivial, deplorable mythology founded on the easiest possible life. Thus postmodern aesthetics in this version can be seen to be registering the euphoric cultural consciousness sundered from its origins and unconscious of its fate. Jencks (1987), however, enhances astoundingly its counter avant-garde orientation by seeing in it the return of humanism. The nucleus of his new aesthetics is the re-establishment of the enduring values of art – an argument which is not unlike T.S. Eliot's paradigm of the ever vital tradition. For Jencks, the rules and conventions are inevitable and desirable. Postmodern aesthetics, he argues, fosters difficult wholes rooted in dissonant beauty or harmonious disharmony. It favours disjunctions, collisions and paradoxes like 'asymmetric symmetry'. It informs the pluralism of juxtaposed stylistic aspects, which culminates in radical eclecticism. This approach feeds off nostalgic or ironic pastiche and the play with anamnesis and annexed mythologies. It looks for anthropomorphism (which is revealed in architecture by function subordinated to narration and the frequency of ornaments and decoration).

When Jencks tries to humanize postmodernism in this way his arguments are ostentatiously invalid. His aesthetic gospel is to continue the old principle of *coincidentia oppositorum* which, thanks to double-coded (or multi-coded) procedures, warrants as many values as possible and enriches their meaningfulness by new tenets such as ellipse, erosion and elision. However, the result is close to a reiteration of the kitsch-like postmodernism Jencks wants to overcome. There is no room here for a genuine dialogue with the past: History is reduced to a mere shibboleth. No dramatic human lot can be accepted and no supreme sense of the work of art (revealed or cryptic) can be of any interest to the artist. The old aesthetic ideas are but vestiges adjusted, as Jencks himself recognizes, to the fast-food commonplace culture. The modern tradition is resuscitated only by the application of high-tech, functional-constructive facets which are arbitrarily employed.

Such postmodern aesthetics clearly severs its bonds with post-structuralism. Its semiotics (if applied as in Jencks' doctrine of double-coded messages) retreats to the structuralist position. That is why Jencks and Lyotard are patently at odds. Each accuses the other of abandoning postmodernist premises. While Lyotard's aesthetics draws on avant-garde para-aesthetics, Jencks' polemic with the avant-garde premises climaxes with a call for the return to art and the continuation of some traditional aesthetics paradigms. His aesthetics resembles a theoretico-practical guide, a kind of poetics which tries to legitimate old principles of art without turning them into stiff canons binding everybody and everywhere. Because mass art, mixed with scraps of high art in a goulash concocted to meet everybody's taste, provides the very ground for this theoretico-practical guide, the latter is neither traditional nor modernist and also by no means opposite to these predecessors. Oliva is perhaps hitting the mark when speaking of 'joyful nihilism' which amounts to confessing a non-identity of the artist, or, in other words, his or her changeable masks.

Of the two species of aesthetics, the second seems to be more adequate to what should be understood by the postmodernist structure of mind. Yet there is no fool-proof theory of what postmodernity means. The concept is equivocal and is often used in quite contradictory ways. I see the basic conflict in conferring meaning on the term as either (a) laying the emphasis on inter-textual games (i.e. the infinite interpretations of unrelated signifiers and the upswing of differences); or (b) concentrating on camp and pop imagery, the merging of popular and classical arts and upgrading of mass culture hitherto stigmatized as mere 'junk'.

Both art and aesthetics succumb to the heterogeneous, fragmented reality which is a set of simulacra. In both it is confirmed that no ordering principles made sense when Reason burst. However, this common negation leads in different directions when it comes to pointing out what is of greatest significance in the ruined space of modernism. There are, of course, passages and interconnections between the two approaches.

Jencks, as is widely known, took over the idea of double coding from Leslie Fiedler. Fiedler claimed that with the advent of mass culture there is still the chance of creating works which will appeal to both refined and average readers, thus combining the demands of the market and the exigencies of high culture. It seems that the writers who met with great admiration and respect – for example, Calvino and Barth – in their theorizing on their own creation and on contemporary culture, expressed views which to a considerable extent continue avant-garde attitudes; whereas their artistic practice flirts in an ostentatious manner with postmodernism based on mass-culture patterns. However, in their novels there are also obvious features of the avant-garde consciousness when they refer themselves to the present-day philosophical and artistic void. A striking instance can be found in Barth's *Lost in the Funhouse* which is simultaneously a novel and an essay on its (the novel's) crumbling state.

The aesthetic thought developed by the representatives of the in-between position is partly close to Lyotard and partly and to Jencks' poetics. None the less, I would say that the distance of these writers from Lyotard and Welsch is much shorter than from Jencks' classical humanism. This is particularly clear in the case of Eco's 'Innovation and Repetition' (1985). Eco opposes the modernist worship of metaphor, the idiomatic, full-fledged information and novelty to the postmodernist rules of repetition, abundance, playing with familiar schemes and expecting messages which are most frequent in the mass media. Postmodernism founded on varying iteration of familial motives and replicas corresponds to the paradigms characteristic of mass culture. However, Eco takes into account not only retakes, remakes, serials, sagas and so on, but also inter-textual dialogue which, by explicit quotations, comments on the creative process, touches upon the death of art and is addressed to a sophisticated, highly educated audience. At this point, Eco comes nearest to Lyotard's position. More than that, he contends that the combination of schemes (*topoi*) and innovations, organized differentiation and regulated irregularity belongs to constant phenomena through the history of literature and art. He mentions Greek tragedy, Sterne's anti-novel (*Tristram Shandy*), Shakespeare, Balzac, and so on. He attaches more importance to the self-awareness of the artist than to the regular consumers who, like children, love the same story being told again and again, perhaps with some variation.

Eco calls his postmodernist aesthetics either 'neo-baroque' or 'archaic'. Thus the specific features of the postmodern transformation in this field become confused. Eco oscillates freely between the two polar solutions.

III

The approach of Jencks and Oliva is the closest one to the postmodern. For postmodernism is the cultural logic which accommodates itself to a new social fabric (i.e. to the world of cultural commodities tied with the digestion of everything from the past and present and the submission to marketing and advertising codes). Culture is administered by media, and the media are seduced by the politics of quick exchange.

Contra Weber, the manipulators are today much less rigorous bureaucrats than the ubiquitous, educated managers. No philosophic-historical blueprints are acquired in this vertiginous society, for no future-mindedness makes sense in the joyful flow of wares. Transparency of being is reduced to a repulsive phantom. Temporality functions primarily as the instantaneous and gives way to many spatialities mapping the highly differentiated public scene. The borderlines between reality and fiction became altogether fuzzy because everything is artificial where signs without any reference are doubled by signs. The human being is immersed in the welter of fugitive images. The labyrinth of spasmodically served signs and dis-

courses ceases to be a mystery: it has become a banal normal-
ity which reproduces itself without any shame or self-doubt
and confirms the disparity and incommensurability of our
inner and outer relativity. Art and aesthetics have to develop
in line with the new dominant social networks as they are,
with the ruling disparities, fun-with-many-faces, boundless
permissiveness.

Contra Jameson (1992) with whom I share an understanding
of postmodernism as the cultural logic of late capitalism, my
position is that what most probably distinguishes the new
cultural mutation in its permanent functional interconnecting
of political and socio-economical and cultural transfigurations
is the prevalence of the circulation of cultural goods and the
emergence of a special class of intermediaries involved in the
management of this type of commodity society. This, I think,
could be the crux of the matter and not the putative causal links
or else strong dependence of postmodernism on recent multi-
national modes of capitalism. Moreover, Jameson dates the
emergence of postmodernism to the beginning of the 1950s
and its crystallization with the oil crisis of the 1970s. In
consequence, all recent avant-garde artists (Pynchon, Cage,
Wilson, Sollers, Beckett, Doctorow, etc.) are counted as postmodernists. This I find a categorical mistake. Jameson leaves
aside the rebellious and emancipatory attitude of these artists.
He forgets about their resistance to the mystifying ambience,
their nostalgic search for principles (in opposition to the mere
retro-attitude in film or music), their schizoid challenge to the
paranoic world (in the Lacanian–Deleuzian sense). None of
this has anything to do with subordination to diversity, chaos
and all-permissiveness. I accept that from Warhol and hyper-
realism one may trace avenues to the openly conformist stance
of postmodernism; but I deny that the avant-garde context of
Cage, Wilson, Sollers, Pynchon, etc. has the same tendency.

My objection to Jameson has a direct bearing on the divide
between the two main kinds of the aesthetics of postmodernism. To repeat once again: the first is ambiguous because
it continues the inter-textual, post-structural revolt and is
stamped by avant-garde attitudes which belong to the modern

worldview; the second is ordinarily anti-avant-garde (anti-post-structural) even when it rests on double coding. But altogether, I find all distinguished kinds of postmodern aesthetics of dubious character. Let me at the end of these deliberations raise the fundamental issue. Instead of asking to what degree postmodern aesthetics continues or departs from traditionally understood aesthetic thought, we should rather turn to the questions: Why aesthetics? What is it for? I agree with Marquard that the inquiry into 'what-for-and-why' is prior to all other considerations, although there is feedback between this inquiry and the routine examination of the subject and procedures of scholarship called aesthetics. What matters here is none the less the possibility that aesthetics could be useful, like all other humanities, or especially privileged because of its role in illuminating the human lot, or as merely useless. Isn't the last option proper to Lyotard's postmodernism?

Aesthetics is meant either to be dissolved into meta-philosophy and beyond-philosophy, or it is meant to gravitate towards the theory of culture which conflates low art with high art and glories in eclecticism. For Marquard, who takes another route, all art and aesthetics compensates for the insufficiency and defeats of Logos in its religious, metaphysical, ethical and historical forms. Aesthetics as the organon of philosophy fails too when it is challenged by the ultimate question of our being in the world without any absolute.

Philosohy, art and aesthetics are aware of the tragic doom of our existence. That is why they have to assent to the comic claims of any universally binding theory primed to eliminate enigmas and dilemmas from the world. Yet the helplessness of reaching the answers which should be settled once and for all confirms the dramatic existential tension and suspense which are felt in the light of inexhaustible eschatological yearning and an unsuppressed search after principles. Thus, it is our human condition which propels even sceptics towards repeating incessantly the same Sysiphian crusade to win certainty of cognition and conscience. In other words, despite critical self-consciousness, the human *Gewissen-haben* still makes us defend, in an ongoing compensatory process, the worldview with firm foundations. The rub is that we solve nothing for sure but cannot cancel the problem. Among other instruments in this duel are art and aesthetics.

I contend that the postmodernist approach in its main versions cannot deal with these crucial issues. Neither paracriticism which replaces aesthetics nor practical aesthetics of the Jencksian mode supports the vitality of the main existential problems transpiring through art and aesthetic experience. Rather, they make dormant the constituents of our human condition which looks vainly but necessarily for the ultimate tribunal. For when aesthetics returns to the classicist rules, its humanism becomes fake or worn out as it confirms only what is familiar; it remakes the established symbolics without any problematizing of our existence. Yet when aesthetics is absorbed by philosophy or philosophizing art then the troublesome questions reappear. Lyotard's *autre-savoir* or Welsch's transversal reason do not break away from philosophizing and it is symptomatic that in the frame of multiplicity the frame of unity, and in the frame of difference and dissent the frame of consent, come back like the boomerang. In any case, I see sufficiently strong reasons not to abandon philosophy of art as it ponders seminal issues of our existence from a *particular* perspective (theorizing *on* art while at the same time *within* it, which results in a fecund dialogue full of tension).

The in-between position, as I attempted to show, does not save aesthetics in its postmodernist mode. It makes us wonder when it returns to the bedrock of the avant-gardist thinking. It immerses and vanishes when encompassed by what Eco called 'archaic aesthetics'. The restitution of aesthetics in that case remains dubious because the ephemeral subject of reflecting upon (the mass-culture model) remains at odds with the challenging subject (the newest avant-garde meditative, self-critical consciousness). Jencks is more consequential when he absorbs the avant-garde (modernist) explosive tenets. However, his saving aesthetics seems to be a legitimation of the rather low-grade artistic practice on the cultural desert. Thus the takeover of mass-culture messages and reaction to them rests primarily on the man-in-the-street.

In Baudriallard (1990) we learn that, as a result of the evolution of humankind from use values through exchange values and sign values to the now developing fractality when all values become contiguous and deprived of any reference in a state of rotary and aleatoric proliferation, human beings lose their standards. This delirious situation is the zero-degree of culture. It is revealed in the aesthetization of everything. All aesthetic and artistic values are denigrated. There is not place for aesthetic reflection; at most there is only a place for the philosophy of culture studying the reasons and contexts of the loss of criteria.

If I am right, then aesthetics is not rehabilitated after the decline associated with the rise of anti-art. It is either done away with or regained in an eclectic mixture of the old canons and the mass-culture paradigms. The wave of aestheticization so praised by a number of sociologists of culture who are dazzled by the social events turned into a spectacle and/or a serial of shop-windows is no salvage of aesthetics. It is mere delusion to see in this superficial carnival of finely packed and quickly purchased goods an aesthetic feast.

Postmodernism constitutes the climax of the cultural crisis symptomatic in our century. The germs of it were evident in the modernist frame but then they were pushed back. Postmodernism, bewildered by the frenzy of pluralistic stimulations, turns the multi-spectacle of our days into self-conceit, promising full liberation from allegedly totalizing imperial modernism. Yet the major paradox of postmodernism is the combination of fear of hegemonic theoretical discourse and of renewed, perpetual theorizing in the form of negative generalities pertaining to the menace of totalization. The same paradox is evident in the status of aesthetics. It gets abolished and at the same time rehabilitated as some peculiar series of texts (discourses) relating to art. But when we start to reflect upon the meaning of this peculiarity it becomes foggy. Moreover, when it is suggested that we make philosophizing on art the tool of rescuing our world of culture from civilizational threats, deficiencies and misfortunes, it is by no means aesthetics which has to accomplish this noble task.

Thus, if my arguments elucidating the dubious status of postmodern aesthetics and my conclusions are persuasive, is not the whole recent pernicious 'sound and fury' around it a sign of illness – the more so in that the illness is taken to be recovery or even renaissance?

POSTSCRIPT

My reading of Lyotard is corroborated by Carroll (1987) who finely shows the French philosopher's road from *Discours/ figure* (1971) to the present day, pointing to his distrust of theory and the tyranny of concepts in general. Nietzsche is aptly analysed as Lyotard's protagonist in his rejection of aesthetic theory which is always an inadequate reflection upon art. None the less, the usage of the term 'paraesthetics' leaves me uneasy. If it is equivalent to I. Hassan's para-criticism (who, by the way, drew much on Lyotard), the term is plausible. If it would mean semi-aesthetic, it would be in this context a misapprehension. If, finally, it is to suggest another aesthetic, it has to be conceived as being a missed shot. But Carroll – apart from my reservation – touched upon a crucial issue which he hardly noticed and did not elaborate, namely upon the paradox that Lyotard took refuge from aesthetics in philosophy but philosophizing inevitably implies theorizing even when the latter is self-subversion by means of art as its object. It is interesting to note that Lyotard's fascinating considerations on the complexities of art-aesthetics relations are confirmed by his article in *Artforum* (April, 1991). There he reflects upon any theory of art touching only the cultural context of aesthetic phenomena whereas art, its beauty or sublimity, is to be eternal, beyond history, with an excess of attributes not seizable cognitively. But if this is the case, what is the sense of philosophizing on the beautiful and (or) the sublime?

Plate 1a Jerzy Krawczyk
Mademoiselles d' Avignon
1966, oil/canv.

Plate 1b Mariusz
Stanowski *Multi-portrait
of Stefan Morawski* 1989,
photo/draw./canv.

Plate 2 Stanowski's quotations are self-explanatory. It is only worth adding the point that he remodels the original so that its seminal form (or colour) is stressed and 'the text', on which he draws is enriched by contemporary elements which do not distort the frame of reference. His series on Cézanne's self portrait is another attempt to reveal the nature of the artistic process. The structure of the original is preserved, but by its subdivision into elementary parts, changing colours, defining the sub-fields of painting by members, etc., the intellectual element is emphasized.

Here the avant-garde consciousness faithful to *Cézannisme* goes together with the melancholic consciousness that today the artist chiefly revisits the roads visited by the great masters and tries to fathom the play of signs which they used and also those signs which are at our disposal now.

Mariusz Stanowski *Quotations* 1986, acryl./photo/canv. – da Vinci
1987, acryl./photo/coal/canv. – Canova
1987, acryl./photo/draw. – Picasso
1988, acryl./photo/coal/canv. – Manet

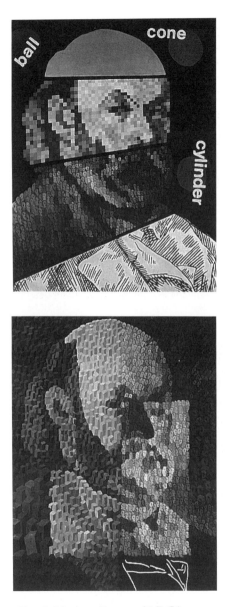

Plate 3 Mariusz Stanowski *P. Cézanne portait* – series 1993–4, acryl./canv.

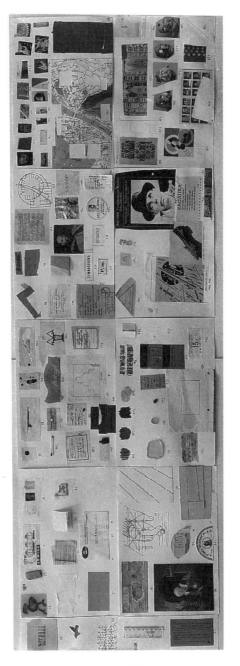

Plate 4a Wlodzimierz Pawlak *Diary* (fragments) collage, 1989

Plate 4b W. Strzeminski *Notes on Russian Art,* 1989

Pawlak employs Wladislaw Strzeminski's vision. The latter is recognized throughout the world as one of the greatest of twentieth-century artists, the founder of the Polish constructivist movement and the author of a new conception christened by him as unism. He was at the same time an outstanding theorist, and his book *Theory of Seeing* (1946) became a catechism for all painters who wanted to prove their intellectual credentials and confirm their dedication to painterly values. However, in Pawlak's case there is basically a subversive tone – Strzeminski serves to open the way back to the classics which must anyway be repainted. Pawlak implies – deliberately – a virtuosic eclecticism demonstrated by the fragment of 'Diary'. However, Stanowski's programmatic eclecticism, artistically subtle and enriched with his own reading of the past, seems to be much more striking and persuasive.

73

Plates 5a and 5b The remains of the Jewish cemetary, Mastaba – wall. A monument of memory of the Tadeusz Augustynek Nazi-victims, Kazimierz Dolny, 1983.

It is worth noting that the rescued (saved) mastabas come from the Catholic cloister which after the expropriation of the monks was taken over by the Gestapo and turned into their headquarters. The mastabas made the pavement of the cloister's court. These mastabas, wonderfully preserved are yet partly destroyed, the inscriptions on them blurred. The intentionally broken wall (in the hole of which I pose with my companion) could be interpreted as a typical sign of postmodernist attitude. However, in this case the a-symmetry and anti-order really express symbolically the lot of the tragically perished nation. This is manifestly clear on the second picture with the row of mastabas in an open space, the testimony to their orphanage now without guardians. I included this sculpture with mixed feelings. It is in my view no typically postmodern piece of art. (I even doubt if it should be treated as an essentially artistic work) but it is sometimes quoted as such and this bears witness to the obscurity of understanding of the idea of postmodernism.

Plate 6a The church of Our Lady of Czestochowa, Warsaw, Lazienkowska Street, 1989. (Tomasz Turczynowicz in cooperation with Anna Bielecka and Piotr Walkowiak)

The first reminds one of a medieval fortress or, if you prefer, fortified cloisters. However, at the same time its fragments, seen from a particular perspective, can be associated with modern secular buildings, say, in the style of early functionalism. The second is basically a Roman church of the middle of the twelfth century, rebuilt around 1760 and now again reshaped in a way which preserves its formal and symbolic meaning, augmenting the atmosphere by the modern structure. I would be inclined to conceive these works as fine examples of revivalism but I have to concede that they can also be described as mildly eclectic works belonging to the postmodern family.

Plate 6b The church of St Andrew the Apostle in Koscielec near Kolo (Poznan province) 1991. (Tomasz Turczynowicz in cooperation with Anna Bielecka and Piotr Walkowiak)

Plate 7 This architect is self-anointed as one of the leading representatives of the Polish version of postmodernism. He is the author of many designs of the type as well as of a very interesting essay on 'Figurativeness and the Decay of Form in the Architecture of the Post-functionalist Era' (1992). His main achievement, the High Seminary in the Kraków suburb of Dębniki shown here, built on the rocks, surrounded by green woods in a mountain landscape, pertains both to the religious symbolism and to a ludic trifling with styles, forms and canons. The symbolic weight rests upon the two-fold interpretation of the Way. First it is seen as the present day continuation of the great historical past, placed on an axis joining in one line the main square of Kraków's old city with its famous churches and the tower of the High Seminary. Second, and in keeping with the name of the whole building, it should be understood as spiritualized space, revealing the presence of the Almighty and the roads of inner struggle to achieve moral perfection. It is to be achieved via four main Doors marking the stages of initiation, hope, knowledge and faith. Particular elements of the project, in line with the idea of cloister architecture do meet the traditional repertory. It is so with the fountain, gardener's house, the court, the library and the aula, the refectories and the Tower of the Resurrection, the belfry, and the cross closing the panorama of the Way. Already in this dimension of fundamental symbolism the ensemble is striking because of its manifold richness, developed by the natural environment, the park with its various avenues and the trees designed to look ancient. The whole thing was planned from the outset for a spectacular effect. The outer and inner spaces are discordant, some buildings are consciously left unfinished, the building material was in many cases left raw. There were planned surprises in the shape of wayward walls, columns hanging from the ceiling, unnecessary objects, staircases which lead nowhere, allusions to the old styles, segments which recall the traditional canons, ornaments in unexpected places and pillars which deny the perpendicular force, etc. Indeed the realization of the blueprint which took five years to grow impressed me as a rare instance of successful dialectics of the heterogeneous, the homogenous, the serious and the fun, the reasonable and the primarily imaginative.

Plate 7 The Way of Four Doors, High Seminary of the Fraternity of the Fathers of the Resurrection, Kraków, Father Pawlicki Street 1983–8 (Daruiusz Kozłowski (with colleagues))

Plate 8 The House of Alchemists, the Factory of Cosmetics, Kraków, Mochnacki Street 1989

The second work by Kozłowski shown here is much more brutal in imposing upon visitors the emblematics of the factory by employing the pink Mouth with its enlarged lips as the chief motif. But the elevation is by no means univocal because the heavy prismal clinker block of earthy crimson colour with four concrete obelisks remains in contrast with the 'soft' walls which look like a semi-face inviting those on the street to enter. The composition is unclear in its purpose: one is not sure what the scale of the object is, what end the details put together serve or what goal the multifarious directions and planes are driving at. Kozłowski's art can be without hesitation named postmodernist; after all, he assumes it as the standard of his creative endeavours.

4

ART, PHILOSOPHY, ART CRITICISM AND THEIR INTERRELATIONS

The postmodern syndrome

This chapter is divided into four parts. The introduction attempts to define what I understand by art, philosophy and art criticism. I know that such an operation really requires a separate book, but my aim here is limited to an attempt to provide a synthesized rendering of some of the paradigms predominating in our cultural heritage for the past two or three centuries. The second part deals with the modern syndrome in the twentieth century and is divided into two subparts: the first embracing the era from the *fin-de-siècle* until the middle of the 1950s, the second covering the period from the 1950s to the end of the 1970s. I shall try to explain why I think it is correct to label both periods as 'modernist' despite the arresting changes caused by the newest avant-garde tendencies. The third and main part of my discussion will describe and analyse the characteristic postmodern traits of art, philosophy and art criticism. One of my questions will be whether the practice of postmodern artists (in different domains and versions) goes together with what is being proclaimed by postmodernist philosophy. Finally, the closing part will lay bare some critical observations about the postmodern syndrome.

I

Let me begin tentatively by outlining what I understand as the pivotal constituents of philosophy, art and aesthetics (which I take here to be synonymous with philosophically rendered art criticism).

By philosophy I understand such knowledge which, first of all, is founded upon totalizing aspirations. Totalizing does not imply a bare embracing of all elements and aspects of reality (Being), but rather establishing a principle or a set of principles organizing the structure of our being in the world. Precisely in this sense philosophy was and is a substitute for religion, either approving God's presence or replacing the divine power by the a-religious alpha and omega.

In this tenet, there is implied an inevitable longing after the meaningfulness of our existence. Even if one denies its presence or finds that the sense of being is always shaky, philosophizing has to ask about it. First of all, philosophizing means self-awareness of the limits of what one proposes. We know only too well that there are diverse visions of the world, competing with each other and all founded on some good reasons. That is why philosophizing is by its very character critical and self-critical. It is dedicated to questioning everything including its own premises and answers. Hence its yearning for the Absolute is always counterposed by the self-awareness of basic uncertainty with respect to 'eternal' answers. Whereas science aims at axiological neutrality (whether or not it is attainable is another matter not to be tackled here), philosophy is conscious of its axiological engagement, its outright dependence on the given individual contact with the historically and culturally determined world, imprinted by the outlook which resides in the subject's experience.

In this sense philosophy comes near to art. However, having said that, it is necessary to add the reservation that the artist's vision is personal (idiomatic) without any necessary claims to universal relevance, while the philosopher has to emphasize the all-binding validity of what he or she proposes as principles. For philosophy, then, there is an incessant yearning for one matrix and a permanent search for an ecumencial language. But both are beyond our reach. Philosophy must live with this dramatic dilemma. Perhaps this is what Plato meant when he defined philosophy as the love of the wisdom which is an ever-receding horizon.

What do I mean by art? The artistic realm consists chiefly in the set of formal-expressive qualities bearing on some special craft (*technē*) which is mostly taught in academies, and on some specific media (vehicles and devices) which define a peculiar ontology (virtual) and a peculiar discourse able to appeal at the same time to senses, emotions, will and intellect. In art, as in philosophy, three distinct and yet interrelated concerns are entangled: the beyond-human world, history at a concrete spatio-temporal juncture and a given 'I'. However, art is primarily if not exclusively concerned with our sense of existence. It can be realistic (mimetic) or non-objective, fascinated with everyday details or with phantoms and chimeras; it can confirm the status quo or run amok in a rebellious frenzy. But with rare exceptions it always bears witness to the bewilderment of life, its muddle and mysteries, humankind's incessant dialogue with itself and the world.

Art asks questions – sometimes clear, sometimes obscure – which usually have no clear answers. Even unambitious art deprived of any philosophical intent uncovers the uncertainty and confusion which often overwhelm us. This is because most artists do not translate into their specific languages widely acknowledged philosophic or religious truths. Rather, they tend to provide a particular private vision, encouraging us to share their viewpoints. Moreover, they make us sensible as much to what is given as to the unknown, ineffable, hardly comprehensible. Confusion is thus the counterpart of life's enigmas and the burden of existence which is authentically human while remaining burdensome (*pace* Kundera).

Now how do I understand aesthetics and why do I treat it as identical to art criticism? It goes without saying that Kantian ideas marked a transformation in the history of aesthetics. Kant summarized and redefined the question raised more than two centuries before and brought to full light by Baumgarten, namely the relation of the aesthetic to epistemological, moral and religious attitudes, as well as common-sensical responses to the world. Nevertheless, this line of evolution was only one of two major influences on the emergence of aesthetics. The second stemmed from Alberti and Da Vinci and was developed in the eighteenth century by Batteux, Sulzer, Diderot and

Lessing. This second strand touched upon the distinctive class of artworks. Here, aesthetics emerged as a philosophical knowledge concerned with the correspondence between specific objects established as works of art and the specific perceptions incited by them. In brief, by the threshold of the nineteenth century, aesthetics was the philosophy of art concerned with the criteria of specific valuations, linked to definite general philosophical assumptions, but to equal degree dependent on the theories of particular art domains. Among the first practitioners of modern aesthetics was Friedrich Schiller. Schiller put exceptional weight on *homo aestheticus*. He stressed the importance of aesthetics as the peculiar knowledge used to describe, analyse, explain and thoroughly grasp the meaning of art. He also laid stress on its potential in the emancipation of humankind.

Of course, aesthetics did not ignore the results of natural science and the humanities. There are many instances when the aestheticians surrendered to the temptation of the promise of fully verifiable measures and procedures. However, every time the promises proved to be illusionary since the questions asked resisted strict examination and the uniqueness of works of art was always somewhat at odds with generalizations. Aesthetics became a specific kind of knowledge founded on the search for regularities which must take account of irregularity, uniqueness and the not-quite-explicable.

These tentative definitions of philosophy, art and aesthetics are based on their relative autonomy and imply connections between them. It might be objected that by defining philosophy, art and aesthetics in this fashion I am trapped in a vicious circle: that is, I tacitly endorse the modernist perspective which necessarily involves the adoption of an *a priori* normative stance. I cannot deny that I have sympathy for this point of view. I find the arguments supporting the modernist syndrome sufficiently reasonable and flexible. But I would say that my perspective does not necessarily paralyse a critical approach; rather, it lets me examine the stakes of the blurring of the relative sovereignty of the three domains.

II

Modernity must be conceived of as a dynamic, expanding process. It originated with the late Renaissance, developed quickly in the seventeenth century, calling into life academies, *la republique de lettres* and the spectacular advances of the natural sciences. It matured in the epoch of the French and Industrial Revolutions, bringing in their aftermath the great social Utopias – among them the Marxist worldview which was clearly to influence world history – and enormous technological advancement. It has climaxed in our own age.

The concepts of art and aesthetics were born and fortified exactly at the time of the growth of modernity. The academy and the galleries, the professionalization of critique, the increasing independence of artistic production from given courtly or ecclesiastical patronage – all these and similar phenomena are interconnected and all paved the way to the emergence of relatively sovereign aesthetic culture. But the fully conscious declarations of self sufficient art and aesthetics appeared only with the emergence of a distinctive modernist sensibility.

Philosophy too came gradually to its identity with the Cartesian *ens cogitans*, Vico's *ens historicum* and Spinoza's and Bacon's teachings. Its full-bloom maturity was marked by Kant. From the time of the French encyclopediasts and the next century it had to confirm or resist the status of *ancilla ideologiae* or *ancilla scientiae*. From Hegel it was grasped as the royal *Wissenschaft* revealing humankind's goals, fulfilling the role of mandatory and greatest functionary of truth. But this wave stopped or was further held back with reservations at the turn of the nineteenth and twentieth centuries. In many disputes between the most outstanding thinkers of the era, there emerged the self reflexion that no solution can attain unchallenged ascendency. Then analytic thinking on one side and Heidegger on the other were the very proof that philosophy has to be primarily self-critical. The consequences of it with regard to social reality pertained to the conviction that there is no fixed order of things once and forever settled.

This, then, was the epitome of modernist information. The regularities discovered by scholars, it was argued, are only circumstantial and spatio-temporal. Progress works in a haphazard way; everything hinges on contingency. The human world is governed by accidentality and innovation. It was added that epistemology is not merely a reconstruction of being; rather, it is something like a schematic map constructed in accordance with given cognitive conventions. Art inspires philosophical thought as much as the latter steadily influenced the former. Kierkegaard and Nietzsche, each in a peculiar manner, were the great initiators of this trend.

In the classical modernist syndrome the relationship between philosophy, art and aesthetics can be conceived as:

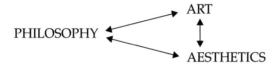

Each exists in relative autonomy. Relative because all depend on the given cultural network taken as a whole. They crisscross and sometimes overlap. But basically each has its own discourse, specific task, function and concern.

According to some commentators postmodernism emerged in the mid-1950s and not in the late 1970s. My own view is that the period from the 1950s to early 1970s is the second stage of modernism. It cannot be denied that the proto-symptoms of the postmodernist outlook and practice were evident then. But they were rather marginal. The second stage of modernism was signalled by the anti-art era. The idea of arthood in its inherited sense was totally demolished. Its chief tenets in almost all artistic domains were destroyed. Form was denied; individual expression was abandoned; the demarcation lines between the self-sufficient artistic microcosms (cognitive, moral and religious) were intentionally softened or eliminated; aesthetic paradigms collapsed. It was said that the art practised since the emergence of the self-sufficiency of the aesthetic realm benumbed the psyche by sheer distilled *Schein*.

Yet the idea of art in the newest avant-garde did not lose its identity. The artist was required to wrestle more successfully than before with the meaningless world. The avant-garde tried to do this by using beyond-art stratagems such as mass media, actions and performances, by deploying a refined discourse extracted from the philosophic or semiotic seminaries and by exploiting everyday iconography, religious beliefs or carnal self-consciousness.

Aesthetics gradually followed, at least partially, 'the artist without art'. Why was this? First, because of the influence of the Berlin Dadaists and the Moscow productivists who had long before rebelled against all aesthetic paradigms. Second, there was the question of the self-examination of the achievements and deficiencies of aesthetics. This examination threw up doubts about the legitimacy of its future. The question was whether it was capable of addressing the most dramatic problems of our time. To be sure, aesthetics might plump for another option, i.e. to focus on strictly natural or divine (transcendent) beauty. But if it were to take this road would it not convert into ontological study? Would it not arbitrarily turn its back on the historical (cultural) world? There was another option for aesthetics: to analyse the effect of mass production on serious art. But does not such a philosophy of art transform itself into the sociology of culture?

All of this showed that anti-aesthetics did not undermine the identity of the philosophy of art. The experimentation typical of the avant-garde spirit became transformed into a series of challenges to the socio-historical status quo. The stake of the experimentation was the question of how to improve the human condition. This concern is shared by the avant-garde of the 1920s and the new avant-garde which emerged in the 1950s. But the new avant-garde took the struggle beyond art. Why? Because the old avant-garde was considered to be over-charmed by aesthetic values and hence instead of facing the ills of the world they established a shelter compensating our hell on earth. Thus the aesthetic-artistic eschatology was doomed to bankruptcy and the existential wager – how to face the scandal of being in general and how to stand the socio-historical evil recurring ever again – came to the fore.

Thus neither the ideas of archē and telos, nor the Utopian designs and the principle of innovation became really suspect.

On the contrary, they were strengthened in the struggle with humankind's misfortunes and defeats, which, alas, cannot be oversome nor even blocked with the weaponry of mere aesthetic-artistic values. The avant-garde ethos was then made even more salient. A parallel movement emerged opposing the philosophy of Mythos to that of Logos. It will do to mention Bataille's heterology, Shestov's existentialism, as well as the works of Gadamer, Ricoeur and Levinas. The philosophy of Mythos rests upon the principle of Eros or the wisdom of Torah or the conversation with past generations, with their 'prejudices' (rooted in *doxa*, etc.) or revelation of something primordial and absolute but of secret character. The inquisitive self-critical attitude here detains all-devouring Reason and re-installs the worth of deviation. The second stage of the modernist syndrome of art-aesthetic-philosophy might be diagramatically presented as follows:

ANTI-ART

PHILOSOPHY OF ANTI-LOGOS

ANTI-AESTHETICS

This is not to say that anti-art and anti-aesthetics determined the preponderance of philosophy of Mythos and the radically self-critical philosophy of Logos. The diagram points only to their parallel tendencies and mutual influences. The crux of the matter is that the identity of the three dimensions was not impaired in the 1950–70 period.

III

Postmodern artists despise or are merely indifferent to theorizing in art. They are mostly as anti-intellectual or a-intellectual as their predecessors were prone to reflect on the status and sense of their activity. Nevertheless, the scene is by no means theoretically empty. The thoughts of, say, L. Venturi or P. Portoghesi on architecture in the era of mass culture go against and beyond the avant-garde and thus are helpful in unearthing the fundamental traits of the new mutation. Jencks did something similar and in a much more extensive manner. Another figure of influence was Oliva, the author of the idea of trans-avant-garde launched at the beginning of the 1980s and the standardbearer of the *Neue Wilde* in Italy and West Germany. There are also many self-commentaries and interviews with such artists as Sherman, Koons, Steinbach and the like, whereas Calvino or Barth voice their views in a highly sophisticated way. If one pays due attention to these utterances and if one examines the diversity of artistic activity in all domains, one can dare to suggest what is meant by postmodernism.

It is indubitably anti-avant-garde. It is indifferent if not inimical to speculations on art's status. Nor does it tolerate any ideological dedication or eschatology (Utopian or emancip-atory blueprints). It questions the pursuit of constant innova-tion and undermines the belief that the best art crusaders are the heroic revolutionaries of the media, means of expression, iconology, etc. Instead, it contends that art is not vocation but one of many occupations. Its legitmacy amounts to producing special commodities which should sell well. It awaits no revolt or transcendence. It insists on the closest contact with the average members of society. The aesthetic dimensions must be restated, either in the dazzling form of the virtuoso fabrication which reminds the stylized art of design demanded by the market or else in the spontaneous expression of the artist who uses colours, sounds, words, etc. disavowing perfection and presenting a familiar reality by some kind of mimesis. In the world without definite axes, in the axiological void, the essen-tial goal is to create freely for pleasure's sake. Classical art and the avant-garde are seen as equally worthwhile tools to play the present-day games. Pastiche and parody are the most suitable vehicles to bear witness to the cultural mish-mash which calls for permissiveness. Its visiting card is unabashed eclecticism.

Postmodern practice is of high culture descent but intention-ally reduces itself to the level of low culture. It wants to be homely since this makes it all the more consumable and so it takes advantage of narration, familiar symbolics and simple form. Its main formula is the pluralization of attitudes and values between which one can choose freely and *ad hoc*. The social reality is approved of in all its dimensions as heterogeneous, segmented, accidental. The consumer society calls for eclecticism and it gets what is expected, thanks to advertisements and the marketing of art.

The *Neue Wilde* group and their companions maintain that nothing today can possess the power of the tribunal and hence art is no mission but a sort of pastime. All principles of the avant-garde are questioned. Even the hyper-realist strategy is suspect because it makes a problem of the demarcation lines between simulation and the possible transparency of the image. No such borderlines are relevant. Painting means only referring to the immediate without any claim to be remembered. The iconography is usually banal or related to the sado-masochistic nightmares of humankind who have no frames of reference and thus can fall back on nothing. The audience's hunger for pictures is satiated either by slapdash eruptions ignoring aesthetic qualities or by masterly efforts which imitate classical predecessors. This outright eclecticism entails disbelief in art's sense of dignity and the conviction that everything is just a commercialized show. R. Longo's images are often borrowed from magazines, newspapers and movie stills. They are seductive clichés on a big scale. Archetypes, old motives and tropes are considered to be no one's property. They become readily appropriated, or rather expropriated, because the historical anchorage does not matter. Painting should always be an exercise using proper craft in order to unite the artist with the mass receivers in their infantile indifference to every serious thought. It should be as comprehensible as graffiti and should, as Oliva puts it, celebrate 'joyful nihilism'.

This form of art responds to market exigencies and so defies the auratic hierarchy of artist values (Benjamin). The self-repeating photography of Sherrie Levine, Mark Kostabi's exercises remaking Léger, Koons' reproducing of all sorts of market icons, Prince's fashionable stylized images, and so on, belong to this category. I am fully aware that the cited artists do differ. Nevertheless, all these works parasitically feed upon the hubbub of ready-made material stuff. In literature and film, as I pointed out in Chapters 1 and 2, the same continuum exists – from the levelling of artwork with mass culture to the sophisticated manoeuvres of Eco or Barth, Allen or Greenaway.

In architecture, average tastes are deeply rooted in the regional (national) tradition and hence it is facile to mistake postmodernism for revivalism. However, the former's products can be discerned by the eclectic juxtaposition of different styles, old and new, reinforced by modernist techniques and brand-new materials. Columns, porticos, arches are re-animated, the space is filled with trees and cascades, broken lines are welcome, colours are invited to co-operate with the shape of forms. Architecture has to be narrative: it employs past symbolics, tries to be funny and frenetic so that it can pleasantly intrigue onlookers. Venturi's famous bet (duck or shed) is sometimes swept away by the supremacy of the iconic over the constructive and the functional. At one end of the spectrum, there is C. Moore with his blatant recasting of remote idioms (piazza) or, say, S. Tigerman's *The House of Daisy* (1976–7), an emblem of the phallus and the vagina; on the other, manifestly refined works (e.g., P. Eisenman, H. Hollein and J. Stirling). They revised radically modern paradigms but stopped short of giving them up entirely. Their strategy is a 'double code' but they too praise intended *bricolage* married to heterogeneity, diversity and the subordination of high tech to the emotional contact with mass receivers by means of definite semantics.

In painting and film, the situation is more pointed and made conspicuous because the postmodernist spectrum here is under the pressure of everyday emblems, advertised by mass media, willingly reduced to easily digestible production without any vestiges of the avant-garde heritage. One can hardly see in works such individuals as, say, M. Bidlo or M. Lersch the prolongation of Duchamp's once blasphemous gesture. They either present the masterpieces which they cynically and ostentatiously usurp as their property, or impudently repeat them and underline the repetition of respected geniuses. What they want to tell us is only that the authorship – even the most original – really does not matter. In a time of serialized fabrication of icons and their multiplication by media, each artwork is everybody's property. When the putting together of old fresh scraps becomes a regular practice of eclecticism, anonymity rules and thus the signature cannot be priced as the primary value. The idea to appropriate the classics as ubiquitous simulacra on the market consists, then, in a legitimate strategy equal to any other. When it sells, it's fine.

If what I have said about postmodern art is correct, one must ask whether it genuinely reconstitutes the artistic realm after the anti-art rebellion. My view is that in the postmodern syndrome art's status is not really regained to its full extent. At one pole it strives to resemble mass production; at the other there are vestiges of the anti-art stance. For me postmodernism is art in a fuzzy state with unclear edges and a soft centre. It is in most cases good craft, but without any authentic artistic claims. It deliberately carries no serious message, no attempt to do justice to the world or contest it. Postmodern production is usually tempered by entertainment and only at its extreme wing, when tormented by self doubt, does it resonate with avant-garde conscience.

Postmodern art is a heterogeneous patchwork, far from the modern self-sufficient art which cherished its world and was attached to the ideal of *non omnis moriar*. It is also alien to the endeavours of the 1950s and 1960s when the aesthetic paradigms were left altogether in the name of the beyond-aesthetic strategy, or for the sake of emancipating humankind. Alas, the effect of this has been a defeat. Postmodernism draws only on such late modern attitudes which accept the triumphant civilization, bedazzled by the frenzy of ephemera.

It is obvious that I take a normative stance with concern to *artistry*. My criteria require not only technical perfection (which is usually fulfilled by postmodernists, sometimes even up to the level of virtuoso craftsmanship) but also on a personal *écriture* seizable in an expressive form and a genuine novelty not amounting to sheer invention. The latter can rest on frivolity which implies that – borrowing Feyerabend's formula – anything goes. Hence my hesitation as to whether postmodernism really comes back to retrieve the *artistry* destroyed by the anti-art movements. The camel of art can hardly pass through the eye of this needle if the main condition of being an artist is being conformist and popular (i.e. corresponding to average needs and tastes). My doubts whether Kostabi, Bidlo, Lersch and others – who parasitize on micro- or macro-quotations, produce paradoxes and pastiches, not in the least embarrassed by the emptiness of their objects – are full-blown artists are confirmed by what was laid bare in a collection of essays entitled *Endgame* (1986). The Boston Institute of Contemporary Art, which published this book commenting on the paintings of Bleckner and Halley as well as the so-called mediated sculpture of Koons, Otterson and Steinbach, made it clear that these artists, while sharply conscious of the civilizational-cultural context in which they are embedded, espouse the ubiquitous consumerist fetishism. Theyare informed by, and subservient to, the demands of malls and the recreation industry. Pleasant possessing becomes the chief imperative of outside urges and art games. Shopping, as openly confessed (e.g., by Steinbach), is the nicest present-day form of tourism and voyeurism. Koons' vacuum cleaners in plexiglass boxes can be interpreted as an emblem of cultural vacuum in general only from the outsider's viewpoint such as, for example, mine. For the artist, one must presume, who presents them without melancholy, anger or irony, they are simply one of the signs of overall commodification and hence close to the desires and expectations of the broadest clientèle. This is certainly also a kind of art but deprived of critical distance, contest, vision transgressing the here-and-now conventions of social and aesthetics praxis. But is it not a mediocre species of *artistry*? Isn't art of that kind too easy and superficial? It can and should be, I insist, the most lucid consciousness and conscience of our difficult lot.

Before we move further, a few indispensable words on post-structuralism from which the philosophically oriented postmodernism in France is derived. There are several excellent books tackling this problem, and thus need to explore this avenue in detail. What has, however, to be recalled is the fact that imposition of a text upon a text, mixing of discourses, the invalidation of any meta-theory as a fixed framework, etc., from which deconstructionism drew its radical consequences, will not do to grasp the postmodern syndrome. What seems constitutive for the latter's statement that no credible grounds (ontological, epistemological, axiological) are accessible and feasible seems to rest on opening paradoxically the doors to the shibboleths harboured in mass culture. What is even more important – the somewhat blurred boundaries between post-structuralism and postmodernism in the domain of literary theory and *meta-reflection* addressed to the latter – become quite distinct when we leave the territory of dilemmatic 'a-theorizing' for literary practice. After all, one can, without any difficulty, substantiate the view that the writers connected with the *Tel Quel* circle (say Sollers and, later, Robbe-Grillet or Simon) remained rather on the other side of the barricade (i.e. the avant-garde tendency with its experimentations with syntax and semantics and bringing the novel to the end of its potential). Their game of clashing diverse *topoi* and motifs, their playing with a polyphonic multiperspectival character of meanings, was the opposite of postmodern writing, partly in the case of Barth, Eco and Calvino. True, they too consciously emphasized the broken substance of language and enhanced the cardinal question of dubious (or patently hopeless) survival of novelistic art. However, from Sollers and Simon there is but a short way to Sukenick and Federman dramatically sketching the impending cultural crisis (or chaos) which the present-day writer has to face. Nothing like this in, say, Barth who gives up the challenge for pastiche and playful flirting with the prose conventions, both old and new. Take his *Sabbatical*. It is based on the motif of the self-consciousness of the hero who is a writer trying to grasp the sense of life – a vain attempt. The novel is in fact a grab-bag of everything, with newspapers, scraps and numerous literary allusions. It is basically founded on adventures comprising sex, crime and espionage narrated in an old-fashioned style. Post-structuralism in its artistic practice had still hidden pathos; here it is deliberate bathos. The writer accepts the ruins of the vocation he or she once followed. Anyhow, Barth is at the extreme wing of the postmodern spectrum where the avant-garde self-sameness has not disappeared and somewhat explodes the *oeuvre*. Thus, one has constantly to keep in mind the factual state of things, namely the presence of different postmodernisms in the domain of art and literature. Philosophical postmodernism is most lucidly aware of these various shades and of its own specific status.

In philosophy postmodernism appears in two versions: first as deconstructive metaphilosophy; next – paradoxically – as thought which has to be already beyond the domain of philosophizing. The targets of deconstructivism are the settled categories which might be called *philosophems*. No substance of being, no divine presence or ultimate tribunal is admitted; nor the pristine beginning and telos. Neither is there an admission of an ethical imperative or a matrix of history. One could say that deconstructive meta-reflection is as much post-philosophical as postmodern. But if all *philosophems* are shown to be mystification what remains? Textual reality, linguistic games and juxtaposition of varied discourses. What are found worthy in the past are forecasts of postmodernist ingenuity. For example, the pyrrhonic and the sophists' endeavours, Montaigne and also Kantian ideas of heterogeneous discourses and his *sensus communis*, which does not refer to conceptual thinking, are appreciated positively. No doubt, too, the anti-metaphysical rebellion of Nietzsche, Heidegger, late Wittgenstein (though Nietzsche with his multi-perspectivism is unanimously treated as the forefather of the whole movement).

Postmodernism maintains that all philosophy is prisoner of idolatry: if it does not search for superhuman Authority it looks for the metaphysical shelter in nature. If these fail, it resorts to human Authorship, whether historical, social or individual. But we begin and finish with texts, without fixed identity, with disseminated meanings requiring permanent interpretation and reinterpretation. The irrevocable conditions of thinking, producing and reading texts are difference and repetition. The world round and within us is deprived of any centre, hierarchy, continuity or axis. Everything becomes segmented and altered in the train of reiteration. Contingency and rootlessness are our world. In the absence of universal principles the possible appeal to solidarity can be only restricted to those who here and there share our beliefs.

The second, radical version of philosophical postmodernism boils down to the following dilemma: If the deconstruction of all *philosophems* is achieved, how are we to describe the thought which suspends all philosophic thinking and rejects it as idolatry and self-mystifying? The answers vary – one is told of pagan and savage thinking (Lyotard) or rhetoric (Derrida) or nomadic thought (Deleuze) or irony (Rorty) or transcendental belletrism (Marquard) or simply weak thought (Vattimo). All these descriptions can be reduced to the results of deconstructionist practice. That means: bringing philosophizing to its limits, testing its aporetic persistence, unearthing the pitfalls of metaphysics which, exiled constantly, comes back. What is positively declared remains unclear. One could possibly speak of another style – essayistic, art-like, privatized views, marked by idiosyncratic choices of metaphoric and aphoristic expressions, etc. But this is not quite 'beyond-philosophy' because this kind of thinking continues modern philosophizing albeit in the vein of Mythos instead of Logos.

It is thus perplexing to read that the hour of genuine philosophizing struck with postmodernism (Lyotard in *Le différend* or Deleuze in *Pourparlers*), or that philosophy is a kind of writing among other equals (Rorty in *Philosophical Papers*). But is that exactly its specificity, one would like to ask? It seems that Marquard (1986) hit home when he coined the formula of *Prinzip des Nichtprinzipiellen* (i.e. the positive negativity has to take the place of what is abandoned; in other words, the counter-fundamentals are opposed to the surgically rehearsed prime elements of being, thinking, evaluating).

There is a striking parallel between the approaches of these postmodernist philosophers and artists. Art in this perspective, although not full fledged, is restored, whereas philosophy is bidden farewell yet returns like a boomerang. However, no less striking is the difference between the two domains. In postmodernist philosophy we do not find anything similar to the mass products. Even the essayistic production is extremely professional. Philosophy, even when radically self-destructive, asks about our being-in-the-world and the predicaments of thinking.

The situation of aesthetics is perhaps more obscure than the identity of art and philosophy. We are told by Hassan in particular that the only nameable ideology of postmodernism is one of accidentality, fractures, intellectual chaos; no paradigms can be supported anymore; no content or hermeneutics or supremacy of form pass muster or make sense. The role of the critic is to undermine definite theory, applying fragmentary interpretations, frames, slippages, montages and such like. Aesthetics is dead: its project survives only in para-criticism, which means in another articulation para-fiction. The critic today, we learn, is a sort of artist, a frame-worker, in love with surprising novelties and unexpected connections, constantly unmaking the aesthetic-philosophical tablets, conscious of ever-changing criteria. Hassan sees no chance of the continuation of aesthetics other than through the subversion of its former foundations – the flaunting of what aesthetics used to be about.

This syndrome may be represented diagramatically thus:

The contours of each domain are unclear. Art gravitates into semi-art, close to mass media. Philosophy is transgressed and becomes reflection about the failures, the dead ends, the vanishing points of all philosophy. Aesthetics mutates into paracriticism. The three domains have exploded and their fragments are somewhat interchanged in a process of constant and unpredictable transmigration.

IV

I shall close with some thoughts of an outsider trying to grasp the new mutation against the background of present-day civilizational transformations.

If philosophizing means necessarily totalizing (not in the sense of embracing everything but subordinating the world to conceived principle), then postmodernism fails to undermine it adequately; indeed it falls into the trap which it tries to get rid of. The beheaded generalizations spring again to the fore. Thus perhaps philosophy must be religion-like, a lay form of asking the same questions. Derrida's *différance* and arch-writing, Deleuze's *rhizome* and *chaosmos*, Lyotard's *le différend*, Rorty's *solidarity* seem to be of this very kind. It is worth recalling Sade whose conception is notoriously considered to be a predecessor of the postmodernist transcendence of perilous philosophies. His critical attack on positive paradigms reached its apogee in absolutizing negative counterparts and turning them into a counter-bible.

Another difficulty with postmodernism is closely related to this point. I refer to the argument that postmodernism is actually a misnomer. No 'post', it is maintained, is valid. Rather, what we face is a new state of mind and a new manner of being within the boundaries of modernism. To put it more preceisely: preconceived postmodernism is to be nothing but a self-improved modernism, conscious of its drawbacks and one-sidedness. But then would it not be more sensible to speak of late or self-corrected modernism? One can argue that philosophy was always built on two opposite trends – one passionately seeking the foundations (an absolute) and another attacking them – attempting to destroy – with equal passion. My contention is that it is impossible to reduce modernism to mere defence of inherited *philosophems* at any price. Just the contrary. Modernism pondered every premise and assumption, objected to absolute certainty, distrusted the far-reaching claims of both Reason and Unreason. Thus postmodernism cannot claim credit for what was accomplished by its nearest predecessor.

What remains, then, for the concept of postmodernism? This brings me to my third objection to the term. I object to the idea of deriving philosophic postmodernism from the heart of art (especially its avant-garde syndrome). Lyotard chose to focus upon artistic examples: Barnett Newman, Buren, Federman, Adami and Arakawa. The critical argument worked as long as

Lyotard spoke of constant experimenting, exploring new rules of creativity, fragmenting reality, applying principles of collage and montage. However, he himself encountered impediments when attempting to impose upon Federman's *Voices within Voices* the indifference towards the world. Federman was seduced by meta-narrative. The same stance is true of Newman. His concept of sublimity is founded upon God's prescence and Christ's Lama Sabachthani motive. The artist's insight into the instantaneous does not correspond fully to what is implied by Lyotard's anti-philosophy. The derivation of postmodernism from the avant-garde appears to entrap Lyotard in sharp contradiction. He confuses anti-art with the new metaphilosophical strategies. True, it cannot be denied that conceptualism as the meta-art provides a kind of pattern for the deconstructive metaphilosophy. However, there are important divergences between the two approaches. Conceptualism was modernist in root and branch (with an exposed or hidden Utopianism). Metaphilosophy is directed against modernism. They tend to try to achieve different goals. Lyotard wants to have his cake and eat it.

As for Welsch, he provides a spectacular example of an infectious optimism. He believes that postmodernist culture means that the revival of humankind awaits us tomorrow. No more dictatorship – political, technological or through mass media. Instead, Welsch sees full sovereignty for the individual and thus full responsibility for a person's actions. His formula of postmodernism states that what was esoteric about modernist culture has now become ubiquitous (ezoteric). For Welsch the anaesthetic, cheap and vulgar eclectic mass culture, which is nucleated around dazzling media and high-tech gadgets, should give way to the sensorium of finally free-winged philosophizing. However, if this is genuine postmodernism how can it be ubiquitous and why is there so much room for ugly tastes? There are no good reasons to enjoy the rebirth of culture.

Postmodernism is nothing but the symptom of the disease of culture concealed and often perniciously transmuted into sheer triumphs of civilization and society after the assorted ills of modernism. My discussion of the false optimism of postmodernism is closely connected with my reservations about criticism of the modernists who allegedly pleased uniformity and standardization of culture. Both criticisms generalize only partial features of the cultural formation of modernism. Aside from the ideas entailing global culture, hence uniformity, there was a tendency to foster as much variety and difference as possible. One could perhaps say that modernism gave rise to the pluralism of quality, whereas in the new mutation it consists of quantity and accompanying flimsiness.

Another charge is that of elitism. One can only reply that there must be an elite and thus the question is: Which one? Where the moderns really the bearers of tyranny and prejudice? Did they impose their pattern and value on the rest of society by force? Is not the elite of managers and narrow-minded experts so much esteemed by postmodernism much worse? Do they not immobilize spiritual aspirations? I am afraid that instead of modernist wheat we are left with chaff in our hands.

Max Weber dealt with the second disenchantment of the world. Now we confront the third disenchantment – the elites are said to be the wrongdoers and many of those who embrace the postmodernist tirades feel absolve of any obligation to protest or to make a counter-move. The disheartening question, *'Qui custodiet custodes?'* rings through the centuries and its knell will not go away. In the totalitarian system the elites were recruited from politicians, security and policy officials, the commanding ideologues. Under postmodernism the elites are drawn from business pundits, technocratic mandarins and super-managers of the mass media. If the approaching millennium is to bear better fruits than ours one must seriously ask whether the now prestigious elite is superior to the modernist elite. The latter was damned for being self-conceived educators. But can we do away with education? How can our custodians go on without guidelines? And where do these guidelines come from, if not from the processes of education, of learning and sharing learning?

My final objection is caused by oft-reiterated statement that modernist totalization implies directly or indirectly totalitarianism. There is no sound correlation between totalizing thinking and political authoritarianism or despotism. True, the Soviet system on one side and the Nazi system on the other derived their ideology from absolutized principles. The same once happened with the Jesuit government in Paraguay. But the philosophies of, say, Bloch and Levinas are counter-examples of unshakeable weight. Bloch was a fellow traveller of communism, Levinas' worldview is based on Torah and strict moral rules. None the less, any student acquainted with the above philosophies has to agree that they are involved in defence of liberty joined with a community for which one feels oneself responsible. Finally, it was precisely the modernist formation which, from Locke through to Mill and Arendt, enjoined a political philosophy denouncing all kinds of totalitarianism. On the other side, from Nietzsche, the stepfather of postmodernism, there evolved totalitarian ideas. One has, then, every reason to doubt whether postmodern democracy offers a better alternative with its mass communication, rapid changes, all-permissiveness, chaos and mind-massage.

The pluralist cultural reality with its uproar of heterogeneous voices rests on the belief that the struggle for equality, liberty, justice and fraternity is obsolete. This condition has undoubtedly produced new idols. Their names are all-pervasive diversity and dissent; they involve entirely privatized freedom without any restraint. For some sociologists the new mutation is or can be the true emancipation. Some even boldly speak of the dawn of real responsibility for one's own existence. No established rules, no fixed principles, no hierarchy, no dictatorship, no elites, no high or low culture – all of this should be like a dose of salts to jaded and exhausted systems of thought. But is this credible? In the postmodern world of all-permissiveness, no freedom is possible and no ethos of responsibility is warranted. Instead, what rules is the cacophony of goods and gross indifference to the lot of others, vertigo from heterogeneous, kaleidoscopic tumult and blindness with regard to values which become valueless. This is the result of the cultural shift which has taken place in recent decades. Artistic eclecticism, its practice of pastiche and parody corresponds adequately to the anonymous, fragmented and motley social fabric which can be encapsulated as permissive consumerism or vice versa.

Is *phronesis* a palliative against *episteme*? By no means. They do not exclude but supplement each other. Aristotle meant to emphasize the importance of the public sphere founded on community as opposed to sheer animal-like labour and the utilitarian values represented by *homo faber*. The ancient Greek idea was to bind praxis with *poiesis*. Humankind as *zoon politikon* had to be harboured in the order of being. Aristotle believed that such ranking of values makes sense. Importantly, he maintained that no artist was meant to be inferior to politicians or philosophers because of his *banausic* (technical) involvements. The task of the philosopher was to express in theory what the politician expressed in practical wisdom. Postmodernists appropriate the concept of *phronesis* for their own profit (i.e. the denigration of *philosophems*).

But is not the idea of the ancient Greeks actually closer to the deepest needs of our spiritual survival? I raise the problem of *phronesis* here because it leads to my conclusion. The modern autonomy of art, philosophy and aesthetics is not an unconditional value which should be protected in all circumstances and at any price. It was only a relative sovereignty which called for an intertwining of the three domains. But there is an enormous difference between such weakening of the sovereignty of the three domains and the postmodern syndrome. In the former, as in Heidegger, it is unquestionably philosophy which embraces art and aesthetics in order to outline the vision of the world and to make it meaningful. In the latter it is the helplessness accompanying uncertainty which causes art, philosophy and aesthetics to become unidentifiable. Does not postmodernism stand as an alarming sign of a cultural crisis in which not only the ultimate answers but also the ultimate questions cease to be self-evident? Kolakowski was right to point out that no ecumenically relevant answers are available in philosophy but, not withstanding the recurrent defeats, we must repeat the pilgrimage to the alpha and omega. Should we not combat the self-satisfied, all-permissive narcissism that surrounds us by waging an inexorable duel with postmodernist delusions?

5

AN INTERVIEW WITH
STEFAN MORAWSKI

Chris Rojek

When did you start to become interested in the subject of post-modernity?

I do not exactly remember when I first came upon the term 'postmodernism'. It was probably in the midst of the 1970s, either in the Centre for Twentieth-Century Studies in Milwaukee where I happened to have the privilege of a one-year fellowship, or else in Munich where I resided a little later as the guest professor at the university. But I did not pay due attention to it; I took the term at its face value as a kind of naming of a couple of things which appeared on the new artistic scene. In turn, my encounter with it in the work of Hassan and Higgins, as well as my discussions with the young German architects who referred to it in relation to the buildings of Leon and Robert Krier, Paolo Portoghesi, early Michael Graves and James Stirling, led me to conclude that the concept meant perhaps nothing other than a special set of newest avant-garde endeavours and embodiments. Thus, I felt that it was superfluous for my scholarly purposes. I neglected references to Venturi and Johnson because I treated them wrongly as a rationalization of mere commercialism.

Moreover, what appeared to me far more important was the need to explain the way one understands 'modernism' and 'modernity'. They were ambiguous enough to occupy me. I was then deeply involved in wrestling with so-called 'anti-art', in its many manifestations, and also in the transformations of the whole culture in the 1950s and 1960s. It did not strike me then that the object of my studies could be a counter-modernist programme. On the contrary, the counter-cultural alternatives, as well as the conformist attitudes (with their equivalents on the artistic stage), seemed to distil the conflicts and dilemmas inherent in the modernist perspective. In short, postmodernism was at that time absorbed in my view by the idea of newest avant-garde which both continued the classical pattern of the glorious period 1905–30 and was opposed to it.

My next encounter with the concept was after much reading on the topic which made me realize that I should not mix up the newest avant-garde which emerged in the 1950s with post-modernism. Rather, I should treat them as opposite tendencies. From this time I have, intermittently, stayed with the problem of postmodernism and found out what a conceptual mess and even quagmire surrounds the concept. To my great wonder some thinkers considered it to provide a refreshing bath! But the irony of this approach is lessened when one realizes that many of them use the concept with different connotations. They can understand by its meaning pluralism, critical attitude, genuine democracy and many similar phenomena which belong to the modernist heritage and which I endorse. Because of the differences of the premises and strategies of the investigation, I was dragged back to reflect on the pros and cons. In addition, the Polish audience grew more and more interested in these issues and they became concerned with my taking sides in the developing discussions. These commenced in the late 1980s and are continuing, taking in artistic, scientific, philosophic circles, especially of the middle and young generations which favour the turn against universals.

Do you detect variations in what postmodernism means in the United States, France, Germany, Britain and Poland? If so how would you express these differences?

Perhaps a defect of my work is that I do not cite many examples from my native country. I was aware from the very beginning of my inquiries into the recent cultural mutation that at its core are definite civilizational changes of the most advanced character. On several occasions, I have emphasized that without the entrenchment in the consumer society the logic of post-modernism is hardly comprehensible. None the less, despite the influence of the Iron Curtain which blocked the flow of ideas between Eastern Central Europe and the West, we live in a global village. Some of the new postmodern ideas were rapidly swallowed or modified in a specific fashion. The Polish newest avant-garde has its own story. It burgeoned from the late 1960s and suffered a state of exhaustion a decade later. Its collapse overlapped with the emergence of the Solidarity movement which concentrated the creative energies in the bed of patriotic and religious issues.

The process in which the postmodernist achievements from aboard were transplanted on to Polish artistic practice had two aspects: one characterized, alas, by mere imitations, trying to prove that it comes up to the standards of the West; and another, welding foreign achievements with domestic needs and expectations. No doubt the first tendency overshadowed the second, but what matters are the latter specimens. At least two circles have to be mentioned here: *Gruppa* in Warsaw and *Luxus* in Wroclaw. All these painters are imprinted by peculiar Polish conditions. Of course, their main inspiration was the new tide invading from outside, but their peculiarity rested on the fact that they selectively accepted postmodernist strategies. For example, the painters returned to canvas, to its figural contents, expressiveness, sometimes slap-dash painting. Their main target was the ugliness of surrounding life, the hopelessness in the face of prevailing junk-like reality and their rather painful distance from the ambiguous, nationalistic and devotional shibboleths. Their obsessions derived from Polish backwardness. These artists, pigeon-holed hastily and unjustly as the paragons of postmodernism, have renowned predecessors – Hasior, Dwurnik, Duda-Gracz, who were acknowledged as the grotesque realists of the tragi-farcical status quo.

On the whole, these artists did not christen themselves as postmodernist, but they did not protest publicly against the label. One of them, Włdzimierz Pawlak, who co-created the *Gruppa* circle can be seen as the representative of refined eclecticism, drawing on the ideas of twentieth-century Polish writers, such as Witkiewicz and Gombrowicz, or else evoking the aura of Mozart's *Requiem* and the message of Malevich. All these paintings are nostalgic but the emotion was expressed in the ascetic, minimal art form. When Pawlak displayed *The Didactic Tablets* in Graz in 1983 the critics accurately observed their illogical structure, full of inexplicable accidents and, as a result, called it a Polish puzzle. The crux of the matter is that Pawlak's conceptions and works are closer to Kiefer's *oeuvre* than to a regular postmodernism. There are palpable metaphysical and/or mythological connotations in his hieroglyphic way of painting and in the void which he spreads on his canvas. His colleagues from the same circle – R. Grzyb, M. Sobczyk, R. Woźniak – painted during the martial law years 'anecdotic' pictures which could be easily interpreted as corresponding to the then socio-political realities. They were engaged, despite declaring full disengagement, because they mocked officialdom and ironized the pathos of national-religious slogans which were the emblems of resistance. There is no doubt that they gave up the avant-garde by driving away from anti-art activities, but it would be inadequate to treat them as postmodernists.

In architecture there is a conspicuous trend of revivalism, that is, the return to the vernacular and traditional native forms which make buildings and living space homely. But revivalism is not the constitutive trait of postmodernist enterprises. It can be seen in several works in Warsaw (like the Łazienkowska Street Church of the Virgin of Czestochowa or the Sobieski Hotel), the Silesian Bank in Poznan and the Church of the Resurrection in Kraków. They are richly decorated, or consist of the alloy of stylistic conventions. Polish architects are anti- rather that postmodernist. They got tired and bored with the dry avant-garde rationalism and refused on the whole to follow CIAC conceptions. There are, however, some achievements which can be partly interpreted as postmodern oriented; the designs of Dariusz Kozłowski and some new blueprints of

Tomasz Turczynowicz and his team. My stress is on the word 'partly' because although the techniques are postmodern, the messages transcend the sheer game of means and media. Let me now pass to another instance – music. Paweł Szymański is aligned with postmodernism. He cites Magritte's shock techniques but at the same time sees him as the innocent protagonist. Many quotations are used to build a deliberately familiar, yet unfamiliar, musical semantics or syntax. Each appropriated canon elaborates with another and so they burst the music narration. For example, in *Appendix on Flute and the Set of Instruments* (1983) what strikes the listener is the collage of kaleidoscopic, expressive qualities (funeral march, waltz, solo percussion, etc.) which remain spectacularly counterpunctual. The same idea was embodied in *Quasi una sinfonietta* (1990) where the motif enhanced in the introductory theme suddenly breaks down. If we agree that postmodernism in music is primarily anchored in the negation of sonoristic experiments, punctualism and serialism, aleatoric and graphic messages, etc. and, from the positive angle, in ostentatious incongruency of styles and conventions, the use of trivial music mixed up with the traditional motifs, immobilizing them or suddenly accelerating their movements, employing *glissando*, parodying the idioms and blurring them, then Szymański is to be counted as a member of this artistic family. However, he insists on the highest possible creative consciousness and emphasizes the unforeseeable or incalculable. He thus locates himself in the neighbourhood of such artists as Eco, Barth, Woody Allen, all of whom I count to a large extent among the still avant-garde-minded intellectuals. With Szymański it is even more apparent since he does not address his music to a wider audience.

Some Polish critics say that Penderecki is postmodern-oriented. Usually his two operas *The Black Mask* and *King Ubu* (after A. Jarry) are cited as examples. However, Penderecki's polystylistics, his reinterpretation of the tradition from medieval times to the Secession, reaches back to his work in the early 1970s when no one thought about postmodernism. And what is decisive here is that polystylistics was an unquestionable feature of modernist music.

In the domain of theatre, examples could be Jerzy Grzegorzewski's spectacles juxtaposing the classical dramas with fragments of operetta, or freely remoulding the masterpiece's structure, or Adam Hanuszkiewicz's production. The latter directs classical pieces with the aid of inserts which refer to colloquial events and signs from the surroundings. The idea is that the response of the audience could be made easier and more lively. Among others, Hanuszkiewcz quite successfully stages *Social Soirée*, montaging high-culture fragments with jokes about actual politics, as well as with commentaries on the various current news items. I have to add at this point that most critics are his inexorable opponents. I am not such a severe judge although this kind of theatre is not my favourite.

In literature there is the novel Z by an eminent art historian, Mieczysław Porębski. It was published after Eco's *The Name of the Rose* and it is of the same character in that it lays bare the author's brilliant intelligence, enormous erudition and subtlety of argumentation. Z tells the story (or stories) of human vanity and cruelty through the ages and contains some autobiographical sequences. Interestingly, it features one important element missing in Eco's masterpiece. That is, it is written in many styles so that eclecticism and heterogeneity are given free rein. Z cannot be dismissed with the conclusion that there are many different narratives here. The author ponders in his own way Vico's conception of *ricorso*, later taken over by Nietzsche. Some critics mention the latest novels of Tadeusz Konwicki as the great artist who, after waving farewell to telling stories, returned to them. But his narratives are of a very special brand. He remains ironical towards himself, to his own originality. There is no room for pastiche here.

The most active in this postmodernist domain are the writers of the youngest generation starting now. They sneer at any ideology, emphasizing the ephemeral state of thought and feeling. Among them, such prose-writers as Natalia Goerke and Manuela Gretkowska or such poets as M. Świetlicki and J. Podsiadlo have already and deservedly established their positions. None the less, no one could say that they represent a predominating trend. Postmodernist endeavours in Polish are not rooted in the native infrastructure and, without close interweaving with the social circumstances, they cannot claim the importance of their counterparts in Western Europe and the United States.

In philosophy the trend is even less conspicuous. There are strongholds of postmodernism in Warsaw and Poznan. In both towns the Institute of Culture provides an important rallying point. Much is being published and discussed at conferences. Books and essays on Derrida are of the highest standard, either emphatically positive or somewhat critical. There is already quite extensive and increasing interest in Rorty. Lyotard has also been brought to light. Bauman is widely read and has a circle of admirers and followers. There has not been much published about postmodern ways of understanding science, although Hacking's and Van Fraassen's views are approvingly debated or refuted. Of course, Kuhn, Toulmin, Putnam and Feyerabend are well known to almost every specialist in Poland, but they cannot really be included in the postmodernist family.

The postmodernist wave is simply tolerated, sometimes met with curiosity, but most often it remains at odds with the main current and against the indigenous grain of Polish philosophizing. It is worth remembering that, after the débâcle of the communist system and the rejection of the Marxist worldview, there emerged a great ideological and philosophical black hole. Many – not only intellectuals – had turned in the preceding decade to the Christian worldview. But after the bloodless revolution of 1989 quite a number of people, repelled by the politicization of the predominantly Catholic Church, abandoned these quarters. What is happening at the moment is the gradual transformation of socio-economic mechanisms, which steers the majority of citizens to think in categories of exchange, market, advertisement, plenty of goods, etc., installing slowly the postmodern consciousness which would like to get rid of any worldview.

What variations in postmodernism in the United States, Britain, France, Germany and Eastern-Middle Europe do you detect?

I am pretty much ignorant about the situation in the post-modernist countries of my own region. I took part in a symposium in Budapest at the end of the 1980s where the young scholars were already obviously fluent in dealing with the intricacies of postmodernism and some of them sympathized with the trend. I remember also that in the second half of the 1980s the Rumanian learned journals contained finely written, competent texts on postmodern art. Not long ago, I met several Russian philosophers of art from Moscow and St Petersburg who tackled the question of postmodern culture. I was lucky to obtain *Ad Marginem* (1983), an annual edited by M. Ryklin. It is devoted to Derrida who comments on his own journeys to Russia in 1990 and 1992 and confronts his notes with Benjamin's, Gide's and Etiemblés diaries. Moreover, there is a stimulating talk on literature and philosophy in which Derrida explained the assumptions of his counter-logocentrism.

The task of detecting variations between the French, German, English, Italian and American forms of postmodernism would mean scrutinizing the native development of culture in each of these countries at least from the year 1945. I chose to focus on common denominators because they revealed more sharply the distinguishing features of the new mutation. All start from Nietzsche and go through Heidegger. However, the distinctive qualities are interesting. Take the example of the German 'New Savages'. They drew on expressionism, whereas in Britain and the United States the focus was more on pop art, while in France and Italy the classical tradition was visited and assimilated. As for philosophy, there are differences between the American and European stratagems: James and Dewey on one side, Nietzsche and Mythos-oriented thought on the other. However, also within the European context there are important differences. In Italy (Vattimo's case) hermeneutics is the frame of the reference, and he tries to propose a new 'ethics of interpretation' (1989) founded on the plurality of universes and dialogue which still could be *koiné*.

Jameson writes in his book Postmodernism *(1991) that 'the history of aesthetic style displaces history'. Do you agree that history has been 'displaced'? What about 'Man, its subject'? And what is the relation between 'displaced history' and ethics?*

Let me focus first on the problem of the subject and ethics. Certainly, there is in postmodernism the idea that the subject has become decentred and has disappeared. One sees this in the work of Virilio and Welsch. This goes well with the postmodern condition which moulds 'I' into something even more mobile and changeable than an inner see-saw or carousel of experience. The Janus-faced individual subdued to the multifarious and heterogeneous stimulations is robbed of the continuity of Self. One important aspect of this is the philosophical anti-foundationalism which undermines the reflection on self-identity as useless.

Whether the effect of it is the loss of morality is debatable. Since his work on the Holocaust, Bauman (1989) has emphasized that postmodernism's biding farewell to the legislator should be accompanied by personal guidelines resting on a spontaneous moral sense. If we accept the decentred and disfigured self, which derives its morality *ad hoc*, we have two possible ways before us: either moral duties are treated as playthings, or they are legitimized in previously not accepted or submerged ways. I think that the latter way is what Bauman aims at in his recent writings (1993) on morality without ethics. I do not agree with Bauman's formula on morality without ethics and so am inclined to say that postmodernism deprived of ethos suffers from impaired morality. What Bauman see as blissful, I find rather dismaying.

My chief reservations about Bauman's arguments are the following: ethics as a set of rules consists in legitimating one's beliefs of what is good and bad and thus providing a rationalized defence of one's ways of demeanour with respect to other human beings. If this tentative definition will be accepted, ethics seems to be co-temporal with the history of humankind. In other words, it is not pre-modern, modern or postmodern, but an inevitable companion of ours. True, its assumptions are always claimed to be of a binding nature. However, modernity produced a number of options from which one could choose. For the unreflexive mass morality was always derivative of this or that ethical code taken for granted. However, one cannot be genuinely moral without internalizing the norms of which one is the bearer. Articulating these norms does not mean proving them (if proof is possible), nor justifying them each time by means of a philosophical discourse. Neither does it imply that one must be blind to the presence of different ethics. On the contrary, the individual has to withstand this difference and show by moral practice that his or her ethical code works. It will not work ideally (this is a phantom) but so that it can compete with other paragons of being good.

The present-day situation has debunked ethics. However, it returns immediately when one has to justify the positive value of one's actions. When appealing to the moral sense in any being, Lyotard and Bauman build an ethical code which is similar to Kant's. The difference is that they reject the possibility of acting justly with reference to the universality and legitimacy of 'the ought'. Bauman says that in each context and each circumstance one must choose what is good acting. This goodness is either arbitrary of metaphoric (morality without ethics), or – if taken seriously – calls for, I contend, legitimation and hence becomes supported by an ethical code. Imagine someone who, threatened by a neighbour in one set of circumstances, forgives him or her and stretches out the hand of friendship in one case, or threatens murder in yet another. Which acting was 'good'? How can we decide without ethical assumptions? I am afraid that postmodern conditions make people act only as if morally. Why should any individual be responsible for his or her moral deeds when his or her ethical space is none?

Bauman assaults the extrinsic 'dictatorial' force of ethics, but what should be blamed is the lack of the internalization of given ethical codes in agreement with human conscience. It is noteworthy that the same problems are evidenced by Rorty's conception of a solidarity which should transgress the private views and idiosyncratic way of life. Why, then, should solidarity be cherished only by a given community and not be expanded to cover members of alien communities? How is one to be in solidarity with neighbours without ethics, and the more so with all human beings?

Bauman, being a watchful, self-critical thinker, realized the traps set by the question he launched. That is why in his *Postmodern Ethics* (1993), he look for support in Levinas' philosophy. But it is, I deem, a futile effort to 'postmodernize' this conception. It will do here to recall the intermittent discussion between Derrida and Levinas, making salient the crucial differences and oppositions between them. Moreover, Levinas, when he dwelt on Heidegger, reproached him for abandoning metaphysics. Actually, what he lays out when fighting with the ontological primacy pertains to ethically minded metaphysics different from the vein explored heretofore. By the way, I am eager to subscribe to Bauman's ethical ideas (they could perhaps be considered salutary). However, with the qualification that I would call them modern. But this calls for a separate treatment. In any case, his inquiry into a code which legitimises morality without restraints implies the question of universals or fundamentals.

The interrelations between ethics, the affirmation of 'I' and the understanding of history are too complex to deal with here. Ethics can refer to sovereign 'I' or to history, or to both factors in their entanglement. This frame of reference is decisive from the cultural standpoint. Being 'I'-minded makes history the background from which one tries to gain maximal independence. On the other hand, being history-minded makes it easier to grasp the richness of ethical options in the modern epoch and the ever-returning necessities rooted in the nature of *homo socialis* as the demands of the cultural order.

The dethroning of 'I', ethics and history are the symptoms of the same postmodernist disruption depriving us of any firm sense of being-in-the-world. Incidentally, I do not quite agree with Jameson's argument that the retro-wave in film and literature is the symptom of an empty historicism. I would counter that the retro look is somewhat nostalgic and thus a genuine vestige of the awareness concerning a value which is missed. We all realize that, while treating history as a dustbin, a heap of worn-out values, postmodernism is unable genuinely to revive the past. Its approach to tradition is highly restrictive and instrumental. No return to sources is approved of, no anamnesis in the philosophical sense and no respect for archetypes are admitted. That is why, too, in its struggle with future-obsessed avant-garde, it does not take the side of enduring values. Museum pieces or archives, etc., are only one of many items in the market games.

Much of your work is concerned with the subject of aesthetics. Now in the West aesthetics has been traditionally associated with elite culture. Of course, postmodernism maintains that there has been an irrevocable mixing of codes. Do you agree? You state that postmodern art is semi-art: could you explain what you mean by this once more?

There are many definitions of art. My main object was not to compare competing definitions of art but to distinguish high-circulation art from low-circulation art. For me, the measure of artistry applies to high art. My next step was to accept modern art with its characteristics as the very frame of reference when I dwelt on the anti-art movements that preceded the appearance of postmodernism. A further step brought me to semi-art. By this I mean the postmodern position which resigns from originality, novelty, personal vision, fine craftsmanship, and instead is preoccupied at best, or most frequently, with the reproductions and replicas juxtaposed in an eclectic whole. But such artistic practice does not cover the whole domain of the postmodernist approach. Because there are also virtuoso attainments within its confines, it is technically art beyond any doubt. But even such messages I find too poor and weak to rank them as 'full-blooded' art.

The practice which does not reduce art to pastime or play tends towards the avant-garde or classical model. I do not conceal the fact that 'semi' is juxtaposed with 'genuine' from my viewpoint and the first kind of art is judged to be the less reliable. I do not know if the currently prevailing trend will persist. But nothing persuades me at the moment that art is about to be extinguished. On the contrary, the recent transformations prove that the most recent avant-garde which sought to transcend artistry, did not succeed. But its defeat does not mean that it has vanished. It continues to exist on the cultural margins. Modern art did not disappear either. The situation is, in fact, multi-sided and multi-layered. The problem is what will emerge in the near future as the paragon of artistic practice. No one can guess. Thus my utterances and judgements are consciously both descriptive and honorific. The rub is that my modern yardstick can be swept away for the sake of another – maybe an equally or even more fertile search after different, historically taken, modes of artistic production. As is well known, since as early as the middle of the last century, the emergence of the popular art encouraged the birth of corresponding aesthetics with specific criteria.

Does postmodernism mean that socialism has failed and capitalism triumphed? What developments in philosophy and aesthetics do you see in the future?

Postmodernist and socialist ideology clash with one another. The first is anti-foundational and it denies the philosophy of history based on what Lyotard called *le grand récit*. This turns the notions of emancipation and Utopianism into grand illusions. Socialism is, of course, the opposite of all this. However, your question also raises the matter of socialism's failure as the background of postmodernism's alleged victories. I hold that the two occurrences are not connected by a causal nexus; they merely overlap in the same period.

Postmodernism springs from ubiquitous consumerism and, in this sense, confirms capitalism. On the other hand, communism declined because of its inability to remedy its own defects. This collapse certainly compromises the Utopia of the divine kingdom on earth because the promised paradise of justice and brotherhood took the shape of fiendish totalitarianism barracks. But whether it should also discredit the socialist ideology which is at the core of anti-totalitarianism is not cut and dried. Why should we assume that postmodernism will last forever? We see the gulf between rich and poor which surrounds us: even the most economically advanced countries suffer recessions. I do not know of any strong arguments in defence of consumerist society which could lead one to believe that wealth will inevitably trickle down to all. Inequality will always fuel people's sense of injustice. It seems to me that socialism is very far from being condemned to death by postmodernism. Its roots are deep. It is entrenched in the hope against hope which is part of the human condition. The welfare state conception appears to be invalid, but the yearning after a commonwealth which harmonizes the genius of initiative and individual freedom with brotherhood and sisterhood, is ineradicable.

It is illuminating that almost all religions converge with the socialist blueprint. The divine kingdom on earth is beyond human possibilities, but the drive towards it persists. One should pay attention to John Paul II who remarked that Marxism and communism possess a grain of truth. That is why I do not believe that socialist ideology is over. It exists nowadays not only in the form of relics conserved in the countries which are moving from community to market systems; it is present in the Western world fighting against the amnesia about modern ideals. I can imagine a future in which the gap between the 'haves' and the 'have nots' is a subject for profound enquiry. Am I a dreamer? Perhaps. Yet I would insist on the sobriety of my judgement.

Can you described for the benefit of our English-speaking readers something of your biography?

I went through a regular, well-shaped and executed inter-war education. Then came September 1939. During the war I worked in a factory and tried to carry on medical studies which were half-legal. Soon I abandoned this for the underground university. I was enlisted as a student of philosophy, art history and finally, English philology. I participated in the Warsaw uprisings. After the liberation I completed philosophical and philological examinations. As a young MA I was fortunate to obtain a British Council scholarship which brought me to Sheffield in the years 1946–7. There I studied courses on English language, literature and culture. Later in London I wrote my doctoral thesis on Burke's aesthetics against the background of British philosophizing on art in the eighteenth century. I had fine teachers in England. If my English is faulty they are by no means to blame. Coming back to Poland I became the assistant of Professor Władystan Tatarkiewicz, an eminent historian of philosophy and later of aesthetics. After gaining my Ph.D. at the University of Warsaw I began lecturing in Kraców on social philosophy and the philosophy of art. In 1952 I returned to Warsaw first to work at the Institute of Art History and Theory, and later at the University department of philosophy and sociology. I returned to the Institute in 1968 when I was relegated from teaching duties because of my 'improper' political views.

This is not the full story, though: I sketch it in snatches in order to underline the rather unquiet life of mine. I did not adhere to any philosophical school until 1948. I was brought up in the tradition of the Warsaw-Lvov school which laid stress on analytic thinking, the clear definition of concepts, elegance and coherence of discourse. The models of proper philosophizing were Wienerschule, young Wittgenstein, Moore, Russell and Richards. I was taught to combine the theoretical, systematizing approach with historical study and this helped to clarity my thinking. My equal interest in philosophy, art and literature made it difficult for me to decide the area in which I should specialize. I chose aesthetics by accident. My professor went abroad and I had to take care of his seminars. I remained faithful to this choice although many years later I lectured on Marxist philosophy. Only after 1948 did I become an adherent of this worldview. It happened at the worst moment (i.e. the moment of the dictatorship of the Soviet version of Marxism). I did then share some of the notorious beliefs in dialectical materialism synthesized by Stalin. I now regard these years as pretty much lost. I wrote a very bad book on the prolegomena to Marxist aesthetics – a book that was attacked for its *proletcult* deformation by a party functionary who was no wiser than I but orthodox and more powerful. It was a good lesson of recovery. I began to understand the idiocy of the system and its cultural underpinnings; I withdrew from theory to the history of aesthetic ideas.

After 1956 (i.e. the Polish October and the de-Stalinization of culture), I entered another stage of my academic curriculum. I returned to interpret Marxism in my own manner. I drew on the Western tradition, not on the Soviet heritage. My theoretical and historical works of this time affirm my allegiance to the Marxist worldview adjusted in a dialogue with philosophers of art of many different orientations. Fortunately, my essays were translated abroad. I became known there as a 'liberal-minded' or 'soft' Marxist, which was no doubt true when compared with my reasoning during my earlier Marxist days, and especially with the ruling canons imposed by Soviet mandarins. In the years 1966 and 1967 I was elected Dean of the Philosophical and Sociological Faculty. This engaged me in acute conflicts with Party Officials because I was firmly independent as to personal policy and most opposed to the then Party-line of thinking. In March 1968, together with a few of my colleagues, I was made responsible for the student revolt.

The expulsion from the University and the prohibition from lecturing and publishing allowed me to pass to the next stage of my intellectual biography. At this time I wrote my *Inquiries into the Fundamentals of Aesthetics* and *Marxism and Aesthetics*: the first book was published in the United States and Spain; the second in Italy and later in Mexico, Yugoslavia and Rumania. In 1971 I was allowed to go to the United States as a guest professor in Berkeley, Boston and Seattle. After that I was invited to the States on two more occasions and I also taught in Western Germany. My main interests shifted to the art world. To be more precise, I became interested in the anti-art movements which revealed the problematic nature of aesthetic paradigms. I began to explore the history of the avant-garde and wrote several essays on this matter, especially the new mutation which emerged in the 1950s. I called it the 'neo-avant-garde' and from the perspective of its inherent aesthetics I dwelt on the shaky status of academic philosophy of art. The books springing from this work were published in the mid-1980s. Philosophizing rests primarily on questions not answers. Already in the 1950s and 1960s I adjusted my thinking on art and culture around some questions raised by existentialism and phenomenology. In the 1970s I gradually abandoned the Marxist worldview, although I remained faithful to its method of research. I inquired about art in its genetic and functional interrelations with the socio-cultural transmutation and I was sensitive to the problems of alienation and the possibility of disalienation. The Utopian and emancipatory ideas which retained a hold, even in the teeth of civilizational processes, fascinated me above all. In the middle of the 1980s I lectured on contract, intermittently at the University of Lodz and then at Warsaw where my position was restored by the 1989 Solidarity victory. These lectures were on Lukács, the development of anarchist ideas in their entanglement with Bohemian attitudes and the artistic worldview of the last 150 years, and on the concept of cultural crisis. I published fragments of all this work, which gave me the opportunity to discuss critically the Marxist worldview. My philosophizing at the present moment cannot be encapsulated in a label: the closest ideas I find in Kolakowski's *oeuvre* and I am bound to say that he expounds them in a much better way than I am capable of.

My main interest for the past ten years has been the philosophy of culture and problems of human existence. My conviction is that the mode of our being and thinking is fundamentally *aporetic*. There is no good which does not potentially turn into evil and vice versa. We are in need of transcendence but cannot avoid being entrenched in the empirical realm. There is a chasm between the two, despite the chance of mystical experience – quite a rare thing. The human condition should be rendered as *animal religiosum* because we want more than we are disposed to achieve. We would like to obtain a perfect order and harmony and eliminate the diabolic forces.

But we realize that the divine paradise on earth, to our doom, is not attainable. Permanent antagonisms, conflicts, disappointments, cruelty and destruction are our lot as much as hope and love which we never give up. We long for a balanced existence – in ourselves, with our fellows, with the cosmic powers – but turmoil haunts us in every dimension and every spot. I would say that there is something tragic about our being which drives us towards god-like or god-near blessed splendour but notoriously suffers defeats. At the same time, we are never reconciled to our repeated failures and stand up to make sense of our existence, contesting the status quo.

Thus I find myself on the roads once taken by Stanislaw Ignacy Witkiewicz (dramatist, painter and philosopher) who saw culture declining but heroically protested against this development. And also close to Kolakowski's idea of *horror metaphysicus* which opens emptiness before us and attracts us by its own abyss. Thus, my approach to postmodernism may be more comprehensible. However, I am far from maintaining that postmodernism has no merits: it does because it reinforces and deepens self-critical awareness of the shortcomings and mistakes of modernism. It gives new vigour to metaphilosophy; refreshes the knowledge that art is animated by archetypes and *topoi*; turns attention to mass culture (the strata of which have to be examined without prejudice and preconception); adds new incentives to reflections on the status of science; denounces the intellectual pundits who thought they were the only signposts of wisdom. But on the whole, I appreciate it as a negative adventure because of its obedience to the status quo. I am mentally goaded by its challenge. I disapprove of the intellectual dance around the New Idols, the dance which throws aside all foundations and worships victorious consumerism, and hence I cannot be a silent observer of the new cultural mutation. Let, then, my struggle with postmodernism be taken as the compulsive response of Don Quixote to so many Sancho Panzas. However, do not the symptoms of civilizational and cultural illness at the threshold of the next millennium tell us that quixotic dissent is indispensable?

BIBLIOGRAPHY

Adorno, T. (1974) *Minima Moralia*, London: New Left Books.
—— (1990) *Negative Dialectics*, London: Routledge.
—— (1996) *Aesthetic Theory*, London: Athlone.
—— and Horkheimer, M. (1972) [1945] *The Dialectic of Enlightenment*, London: New Left Books.
Altizer, T. J. *et al.* (eds) (1982) *Deconstruction and Theology*, London: Crossroad Publishing Company.
Ankersmit, F. (1983) *Narrative Logic: A Semantic Analysis of the Historian's Language*, Dordrecht: Kluwer.
Appignanensi, C. and Bennington, G. (eds) (1986) *Postmodern Documents 4*, London: Institute of Contemporary Arts.
Arac, J. (ed.) (1987) *Postmodernism and Politics*, Minnesota: University of Minnesota Press.
Bataille, G. (1970–9) *Oeuvres completes*, Paris: Gallimard.
Baudrillard, J. (1968) *La societé des objets*, Paris: Gallimard.
—— (1970) *La societé de consommation*, Paris: Denoël-Gonthier.
—— (1972) *Pour une critique de l'économie politique du signe*, Paris: Gallimard.
—— (1973) *Le mirroir de la production*, Paris : Casterman.
—— (1976) *L'échange symbolique et la mort*, Paris: Gallimard.
—— (1977) *L'effet Bauboug: implosion et dissuasion*, Paris: Galilée.
—— (1978) *A l'ombre des majorités silencieuses ou la fin du social*, : Fontenay-sous-Bois.
—— (1979) *De la seduction*, Paris: Galilée.
—— (1981) *Simulacres et simulation*, Paris: Galilée.
—— (1983) *Les stratégies fatales*, Paris: Grasset.
—— (1985) *La gauche divine*, Paris: Grasset.
—— (1986)*Amérique*, Paris: Grasset.
—— (1987) *Cool Memories (1980–5)*, Paris: Galilée.
—— (1990) *La transparence du mal*, Paris: Galilée.

—— (1992) *Selected Writings*, ed. M. Poster, 4th edn, Cambridge: Polity Press.

Bauman, Z. (1987) *Legislators and Interpreters: On Modernity, Postmodernity and Intellectuals*, Cambridge: Polity Press.

—— (1989) *Modernity and the Holocaust*, Ithaca: Cornell University Press.

—— (1991) *Modernity and Ambivalence*, Cambridge: Polity Press.

—— (1992a) *Intimations of Postmodernity*, London: Routledge.

—— (1992b) *Mortality, Immortality and Other Life Stragies*, Oxford: Blackwell.

—— (1993) *Post-modern Ethics*, Oxford: Blackwell.

Baynes, K. *et al.* (1987) *Philosophy: End or Transformation?*, Cambridge, MA: MIT Press.

Beck, U. (1985) *Risikogesselschaft: Auf dem Wege in eine andere Moderne*, Frankfurt/M.: Suhrkamp.

—— (1988) *Gegengifte: Die organisierte Unverantworlichkeit*, Frankfurt/M.: Suhrkamp.

Bell, D. (1973) *The Coming of Post-industrial Society: A Venture in Social Forecasting*, New York: Basic Books.

—— (1976) *The Cultural Contradictions of Capitalism*, New York: Basic Books.

—— (1988) *The Winding Passage: Essays and Sociological Journeys, 1960–1980*, New York: Transaction.

Benamou, M. and Caramello, C. (1977) *Performance in Postmodern Culture*, Madison: Coda Press.

Bennington, G. (1988) *Lyotard: Writing the Event*, Manchester: Manchester University Press.

—— and Derrida, J. (1991) *Jaques Derrida*, Paris.

Berman, M. (1983) *All That is Solid Melts into Air: The Experience of Modernity*, London: Verso.

Bernstein, R. (1986) *Philosophical Profiles*, Cambridge: Polity Press.

—— (1991) *The New Constellations*, Oxford.

Best, S. and Kellner, D. (1991) *Postmodern Theory, Critical Interogations*, New York: Guilford Press.

Bloom, H., Hartman, G. and Miller Hillis, J. (1982) *Deconstruction and Criticism*, London/New York: Continuum.

Blumenberg, H. (1966) *Legitimität der Neuzeit*, Frankfurt/M.: Suhrkamp.

Bourdieu, P. (1979) *La distinction: Critique sociale du jugement*, Paris: Minuit.

—— (1992) *Les règles de l'art*, Paris: Seuil.

Bouveresse, J. (1984) *Rationalisme et cynisme*, Paris.

Bradbury, M. and McFarlaine, J. (1976) *Modernism 1890–1930*, Harmondsworth: Penguin.

Brunette, P. and Wills, D. (eds) (1994) *Deconstruction and the Visual Arts: Art Media, Architecture*, Cambridge: Cambridge University Press.

Brunkhorst, H. (1990) *Der entzauberte Intellektuelle: Über die neue Beliebigkeit des Denkens*, Hamburg.

BIBLIOGRAPHY

Bürger, P. (1983) *Theorie der Avantgarde*, Frankfurt/M.: Suhrkamp.
—— and Ch (1987) *Postmoderne, Alltag, Allegorie und Avantgarde*, Frankfurt/M.: Suhrkamp.
Burgin, V. (1986) *The End of Art Theory: Criticism and Postmodenity*, London: Macmillan Press.
Calinescu, M. (1987) *Five Faces of Modernity: Modernism, Avant-Garde, Decadence, Kitsch, Postmodernism*, Durham: Duke University Press.
Callinicos, A. (1989) *Against Postmodernism: A Marxist Critique*, Cambridge: Polity Press.
Caramello, C. (1983) *Silverless Mirrors: Book, Self and Postmodern American Fiction*, Tallahassee: Florida State University Press.
Carrol, D. (1987) *Paraaesthetics: Foucault, Lyotard, Derrida*, New York: Methuen.
Castoriadis, C. (1990) *Le monde morcelé*, Paris: Seuil.
Clair, J. (1983) *Considérations sur l'état des beaux arts*, Paris.
Cometti, J.-P. (ed.) (1992) *Lire Rorty: Le pragmatisme et ses consequences*, Paris: L'eclat.
Cox, H. (1969) *The Feast of Fools: A Theological Essay on Festivity and Fantasy*, Cambridge, MA: Harvard University Press.
—— (1984) *Religion in the Secular City: Toward a Postmodern Theology*, New York: Simon & Schuster.
Crook, S. (1991) *Modernist Radicalism and its Aftermath*, London: Routledge.
——, Pakulski, J. and Waters, M. (1992) *Postmodernisation: Change in Advanced Society* London: Sage.
Davidson, D. (1984) *Inquiries into Truth and Interpretation*, Oxford: Oxford University Press.
Davis, D. (1977) *Artculture: Essays on Postmodernism*, New York: Harper & Row.
Deleuze, G. (1962) *Nietzsche et la philosophie*, Paris: PUF.
—— (1966) *Le bergsonisme*, Paris: PUF.
—— (1968) *Différence et répétition*, Paris: PUF.
—— (1969) *Logique du sens*, Paris: Minuit.
—— (1985) [1983] *Cinéma*, Paris: Minuit.
—— (1986) *Foucault*, Paris: Minuit.
—— and Guattari, F. (1972) *L'anti-Oedipe: Capitalisme et schizophrénie*, Paris: Minuit.
—— (1980) *Mille Plateaux*, Paris: Minuit.
—— (1991) *Qu'est-ce que la philosophie?*, Paris: Minuit.
Derrida, J. (1972a) *La dissémination*, Paris: Seuil.
—— (1972b) *Positions*, Paris: Minuit.
—— (1972c) *Marges de la philosophie*, Paris: Minuit.
—— (1978) *La vérité en peinture*, Paris: Flammarion.
—— (1980) *La Carte Postale. De Socrate à Freud et au-delà*, Paris: Flammarion.
—— (1981a) 'Entretien avec J. Derrida', in *Le Monde*, 31 January.

—— (1981b) *Le fins de l'homme: A partir du travail de Derrida*, Paris: Galilée.
—— (1982a) 'Interview with Ch. V. McDonald', in *Diacritics* XII.
—— (1982b) *Derrida and Biblical Studies*, ed. R. Detweiler, : Chico.
—— (1992) *Derrida: A Critical Reader*, ed. D. Wood, Oxford: Blackwell.
—— *et al.* (1985) *La faculté de juger*, Paris: Minuit.
Dews, P. (1987) *Logics of Disintegration: Post-structuralist Thought and the Claims of Literary Theory*, London: Verso.
Eagleton, T. (1983) *Literary Theory: An Introduction*, Oxford: Blackwell.
—— (1985) *Against the Grain: Selected Essays 1975–85*, London: Verso.
—— (1990) *The Ideology of the Aesthetic*, Oxford: Blackwell.
Eco, U. (1979) *The Role of the Reader*, Bloomington: Indiana University Press.
—— (1984) *Postscript to 'The Name of the Rose'*, San Diego/New York/London: Harcourt Brace Jovanovich.
—— (1985) 'Innovation and Repetition: Between Modern and Post-modern Aesthetics', in *Daedalus*, Fall.
—— (1986) *Travels in Hyperreality*, San Diego/New York/London: Harcourt Brace Jovanovich.
—— (1989) *The Aesthetics of Chaosmos*, Cambridge, MA: Harvard University Press.
—— (1992) *Interpretation and Overinterpretation (The Tanner Lectures)*, Cambridge: Cambridge University Press.
—— (1994) *Six Walks in the Fictional Woods*, Cambridge, MA/London: Cambridge University Press.
Elster, J. (1986) *Sour Grapes: Studies in the Subversion of Rationality*, Cambridge: Cambridge University Press.
—— (1991) *Salomonic Judgements: Studies in the Limitations of Rationaity*, Cambridge: Cambridge University Press.
Endgame (1986) (a collection of essays), Boston: Institute of Contemporary Art.
Etzioni, A. (1968) *The Active Society: A Theory of Societal and Political Processes*, London/New York:.
Featherstone, M. (1991) *Consumer Culture and Postmodernism*, London: Sage.
Federman, R. (1981) *Surfiction: Fiction New and Tomorrow*, Chicago: Swallow Press.
Fekete, J. (ed.) (1987) *Life After Postmodernism*, Manchester: Manchester University Press.
Feyerabend, P. (1975) *Against Method: Outline of Anarchistic Theory of Knowledge*, London: New Left Books.
Fiedler, L. (1970–1) *The Collected Essays*, 2 vols, New York.
Finkielkraut, A. (1987) *Le defaite de la pensée*, Paris.
Fish, S. (1980) *Is There a Text in this Class? Authority of Interpretive Community*, Cambridge, MA: Harvard University Press.
—— (1989) *Doing What Comes Naturally*, Oxford: Claredon.

Fokemma, D. and Bertens, H. (1986) *Approaching Postmodernism*, Amsterdam: John Benjamins.

Forthomme, B. (1979) *Une philosophie de la transcendance: La métaphysique de E. Levinas*, Paris.

Foster, H. (ed.) (1985) *The Postmodern Culture*, London: Pluto Press.

Foucault, M. (1965) [1961] *Folie et déraison: Histoire de la folie à l'age classique*, Paris: Roussell.

—— (1966) *Les mots et les choses: Une archéologie des sciences humaines*, Paris: Gallimard.

—— (1969) *L'archéologie du savoir*, Paris: Gallimard.

—— (1973) *Ceci n'est pas une pipe*, Paris: Montpellier.

—— (1975) *Surveiler et punir: Naisance de la prison*, Paris: Gallimard.

—— (1976–84) *Histoire de la sexualité*, 3 vols, Paris: Gallimard.

—— (1986a) *The Foucault Reader*, ed. P. Rabinow, Harmondsworth: Penguin.

—— (1986b) *Foucault: A Critical Reader*, ed. D. C. Hoy, Oxford: Blackwell.

Fraasen, B. C. Van (1980) *The Scientific Image*, Oxford: Oxford University Press.

Frampton, K. J. (ed.) (1982) *Modern Architecture and the Critical Present*, London: Thames & Hudson.

Frank, M. (1983) *Was ist Neostrukturallismus?*, Frankfurt/M.: Suhrkamp.

—— (1988a) *Die Frage nach dem Subjekt*, Frankfurt/M.: Suhrkamp.

—— (1988b) *Die Grenzen der Verständigung*, Frankfurt/M.: Suhrkamp.

Frankarts, A. (ed.) (1984) *Seduced and Abandoned: The Baudrillard Scene*, Stonemoss Services.

Frisby, D. (1985) *Fragments of Modernity*, Cambridge: Polity Press.

Fukuyama, F. (1992) *The End of History and the Last Man*, New York: Free Press.

Fuller, P. (1988) *Theoria: Art and the Absence of Grace*, London: Chatto & Windus.

Funk, R. (1989) *Sprache und Transzendenz im Denken von E. Levinas*, Munich:.

Gablik, S. (1984) *Has Modernism Failed?*, New York: Thames & Hudson.

Gane, M. (1992) *Baudrillarde's Bestiary: Baudrillard and Culture*, London: Routledge.

Gasché, R. (1986) *The Tain of the Mirror: Derrida and the Philosophy of Reflection*, Cambridge, MA.

Gauchet, M. (1985) *Le disenchantment du monde: Une histoire politique de la réligion*, Paris.

Gehlen, A. (1986) *Zeit-Bilder. Zur Soziologie und Ästhetik der modernen Malerei*, Frankfurt/M.: Suhrkamp.

Gellner, E. (1992) *Reason and Culture*, London: Blackwell.

Giddens, A. (1990) *The Consequences of Modernity*, Oxford: Polity Press.

Habermas, J. (1963) *Theorie und Praxis*, Frankfurt/M.: Suhrkamp.

—— (1968) *Erkenntnis und Interesse*, Neuwied.

—— (1970) *Technik und Wissenschaft als 'Ideologie'*, Frankfurt/M.: Suhrkamp.

—— (1985a) *Der philosophische Diskurs der Moderne*, Frankfurt/M.: Suhrkamp.

—— (1985) *Die neue Unübersichtlichkeit*, Frankfurt/M.: Suhrkamp.

Hacking, J. (1975) *The Emergence of Probability*, Cambridge: Cambridge University Press.

—— (1983) *Representing and Intervening*, Cambridge: Cambridge University Press.

—— (1990) *The Taming of Chance*, Cambridge: Cambridge University Press.

Hall, D. C. (1994) *R. Rorty: Prophet and Poet of the New Pragmatism*, New York: SUNY Press.

Hartman, G. (1981) *Saving the Text: Literature/Derrida/Philosophy*, Baltimore: Baltimore University Press.

Harvey, D. (1989) *The Condition of Postmodernity*, Oxford: Blackwell.

Hassan, I. (1980) *The Right Promethean Fire: Imagination, Science and Cultural Change*, Urbana: University of Illinois Press.

—— (1985) *Paracriticisms: Seven Speculations of the Time*, Urbana: University of Illinois Press.

—— ((1987) *The Postmodern Turn: Essays in Postmodern Theory and Culture*, Columbus: Ohio State University Press.

—— and Hassan, S. (eds) (1983) *Innovation/Renovation: New Perspective in the Humanities*, Madison: University of Wisconsin Press.

Hebdige, D. (1988) *Hiding in the Light: On Images and Things*, London: Routledge.

Heller, A. (1990) *Can Modernism Survive?*, Cambridge: Polity Press.

Heller, A. and Feher, F. (1988) *The Postmodern Political Condition*, Cambridge: Polity Press.

—— (1993) *The Grandeur and Twilight of Radical Universalism*, New Brunswick: Transaction Press.

Herf, J. (1984) *Reactionary Modernism: Technology, Culture and Politics in Weimar and the Third Reich*, Cambridge: Cambridge University Press.

Higgins, R. C. (1978) *A Dialectic of Centuries*, New York.

Hiley, D. R. (1985) *Philosophy in Question*, Chicago: Chicago University Press.

Hobson, M. (1987) *Jacques Derrida*, London.

Horkheimer, M. (1974) *Eclipse of Reason*, New York: Continuum.

—— (1967) *Zur Kritik der instrumentellen Vernunft*, Frankfurt/M.: Suhrkamp.

Hutcheon, L. (1985) *A Theory of Parody: The Teachings of Twentieth-century Art Form*, New York:.

—— (1988) *A Poetics of Postmodernism: History, Theory, Fiction*, New York: Routledge.

Huyssen, A. (1986) *After the Great Divide: Modernism, Mass Culture and Postmodernism*, London: Macmillan.

Huyssen, A. and Scherpe, K. (eds) (1986) *Postmoderne: Zeichen eines kulturellen Wandels*, Hamburg.

Inglis, F. (1988) *Popular Culture and Political Power*, London: Harvester Wheatsheaf.

—— (1990) *Media Theory*, Oxford: Blackwell.

Jameson, F. (1991) *Postmodernism or the Cultural Logic of Late Capitalism*, Durham: Duke University Press.

Jay, M. (1988) *Fin de siècle Socialism and Other Essays*, New York/ London: Routledge.

—— (1993) *Downcast Eyes: The Denigration of Vision in Twentieth-Century French Thought*, Berkeley: University of California Press.

Jencks, C. (1977) *The Language of Post-modern Architecture*, 5th edn, London: Academy Editions.

—— (1980) *Late Modern Architecture*, London/New York: Academy Editions.

—— (1985) *Towards a Symbolic Architecture: The Thematic House*, London: Academy Editions.

—— (1986) *What is Postmodernism?*, London: Academy Editions.

—— (1987) *Post-modernism: The New Classicism in Art and Architecture*, New York: Rizzoli Inc.

Kamper, D. and Van Reyen, W. (eds) (1987) *Die unvollendete Vernunft: Moderne versus Postmoderne*, Frankfurt/M.: Suhrkamp.

Kamuf, P. (ed.) (1991) *The Derrida Reader*, New York: Columbia University Press.

Kellner, D. (1988) *Jean Baudrillard: From Marxism to Postmodernism and Beyond*, Oxford/Cambridge: Polity Press.

—— (ed.) (1989) *Postmodernism/Jameson/Critique*, Washington, DC: Maisonneuve.

Kemper, P. (ed.) (1988) *'Postmoderne' oder der Kampf um die Zukunft*, Frankfurt/M.: Suhrkamp.

Klinkowitz, J. (1985) *Literary Subversions: New American Fiction and the Practice of Criticism*, Carbondale: South Illinois University Press.

Klossowski, P. (1967) *Sade mon prochain*, Paris: Seuil.

—— (1969) *Nietzsche et le circle vicieux*, Paris: Mercure de France.

Klotz, H. (1984) *Die neuen Wilden in Berlin*, Stuttgart.

—— (1987) *Moderne und Postmoderne: Architektur der Gegenwart 1960–1980*, Braunschweig.

Kołakowski, L. (1988) *Metaphysical Horror*, Oxford: Blackwell.

Kondylis, P. (1991) *Der Niedergang der bürgerlichen Denk- und Lebensform: Die liberale Moderne und die massendemokratische Postmoderne*, Weinheim:.

Kosłowski, P. (1988) *Die postmoderne Kultar: Gesellschaftlich-kulturelle Konsequenzen der technischen Entwicklung*, Munich:.

Kroker, A. (1989) *Panic Encyclopedia*, New York: St Martin's Press.

127

—— (1992) *The Possessed Individual, Technology and Postmodernity,* New York: St Martin's Press.
—— and Cook, D. (1986) *The Postmodern Scene: Excremental Culture and Hyper-aesthetics,* New York: St Martin's Press.
Kundera, M. (1986) *L'art du roman,* Paris.
Küng, H. (1990) *Projekt Weltethos,* Tübingen.
Lacou-Labarthe, P. (1990) *Heidegger, Art and Politics,* Oxford: Blackwell.
Lash, S. (1987) *The End of Organized Capitalism,* Cambridge: Polity Press.
—— (1990) *Sociology of Postmodernism,* London: Routledge.
Laub Coser, R. (1991) *In Defense of Modernity: Role Complexity and Individual Autonomy,* Stanford, CA: Stanford University Press.
Lawson, H. and Apignanensi, L. (eds) (1989) *Dismantling Truth: Reality in the Postmodern World,* London: Weidenfeld & Nicholson.
Lehman, D. (1991) *Signs of the Times: Deconstruction and the Fall of P. de Man,* New York: Poseidon.
Leitch, V. B. (1983) *Deconstructive Criticism: An Advanced Introduction,* London:.
Levinas, E. (1947) *De l'existance a l'existant,* Paris:.
—— (1961) *Totalité et infini: Essais sur l'extériorité,* The Hague: Holland.
—— (1968) *Quatre lectures talmudiques,* Paris:.
—— (1974) *Autrement qu'étre ou au delà de l'essence,* The Hague: Kluwer.
—— (1979) *Le temps et l'autre,* Paris.
—— (1982) *De Dieu que vient á l'idée,* Paris.
—— (1991) *Entre nous: Essai sur le penser-á-autrui,* Paris.
Lipovetsky, G. (1983) *L'ère du vide,* Paris: Gallimard.
—— (1987) *L'empire de l'éphémère: Le mode et son destin dans les societés modernes,* Paris: Gallimard.
Llewelyn, J. (1986) *Derrida and the Threshold of Sense,* London: Macmillan.
Lyotard, J. F. (1971) *Discours, figure,* Paris: Klinksieck.
—— (1973a) *Dérivé à partir de Marx et Freud,* Paris: Union générale d'éditions.
—— (1973b) *Des dispositifs pulsionnels,* Paris: Union générale d'éditions.
—— (1974) *Economie libidinale,* Paris: Minuit.
—— (1977a) *Les transformateurs Duchamp,* Paris Galilée.
—— (1977b) *Instructions païennes,* Paris: Galilée.
—— (1977c) *Rudiments païens,* Paris: Union générale d'éditions.
—— (1979) *La condition postmoderne,* Paris: Minuit.
—— (1984a) *Le différend,* Paris: Minuit.
—— (1984b) *Tombeau de l'intellectuel et autres papiers,* Paris: Galilée.
—— (1984c) *Les immateriaux,* Paris: Centre Pompidou.
—— (1986) *Le postmoderne expliqué aux enfants,* Paris: Galilée.
—— (1988a) *Heidegger et les Juifs,* Paris: Galilée.
—— (1988b) *L'inhumain: Causeries sur le temps,* Paris: Galilée.
—— (1989a) *Temoigner du différend: Quand phraser ne se peut* (l'entretien

du centre Sevres, 1987, sous la direction de P.-J. Labarrière, et des exposés par F. Guibal et J. Rogozinski), Paris: Osiris.

—— (1989b) *The Lyotard Reader*, ed. A. Benjamin, Oxford: Blackwell.

—— and Buren, D. (1982) *Le travail et l'écrit chez Daniel Buren*, Paris: Centre Pompidou.

—— and Monory, J. (1977) *Récits tremblants*, Paris: Galilée.

—— (1984) *L'assassinat de l'expérience par la peinture*, Paris: Le Castor Astral.

—— and Thebaud, J. L. (1979) *Au juste*, Paris: Bourgeois.

McHale, B. (1987) *Postmodernist Fiction*, London: Methuen.

Maffesoli, M. (1988) *La temps des tribus: Le declin de l'individualisme dans les societés de masse*, Paris: Klinksieck.

—— (1992) *La transfiguration du politique: La tribalisation du monde*, Paris: Grasset.

Malachowski, A. (ed.) (1990) *Reading Rorty*, Oxford: Blackwell.

Mandel, E. (1975) *Late Capitalism*, London: New Left Books.

Man, P. de (1979) *Allegories of Reading*, New Haven, CN: Yale University Press.

—— (1983) *Blindness and Insight*, London: Routledge.

—— (1986) *The Resistance to Theory*, Manchester: Manchester University Press.

Margolis, J. (1989) *Text without Referents: Reconciling Science and Narratives*, Oxford: Blackwell.

Marquard, O. (1981) *Abschied vom Prinzipiellen*, Stuttgart: Reclam.

—— (1986) *Apologie des Zufälligen*, Stuttgart: Reclam.

—— (1989) *Aesthetica und Anaesthetica, Philosophische Uberlegungen*, Schöningh: Paderborn.

Melville, S. (1986) *Philosophy Besides Itself. On Deconstruction and Postmodernism*, Minneapolis: University of Minnesota Press.

Mestrovic, S. G. (1992) *Durkheim and Postmodern Culture*, New York: Hawthorne.

——, Goreta, M. and Letica, S. (1993) *The Road from Paradise*, Lexington: University of Kentucky.

Miller, J. H. (1987) *The Ethics of Reading*, New York: Columbia University Press.

Murphy, J. W. (1989) *Postmodern Social Analysis and Criticism*, New York: Greenwood.

Newman, C. (1985) *The Postmodern Aura. The Age of Fiction in the Age of Inflation*, Evanston: Northwestern University Press.

Netzhammer, L. (1984) *Posthistoire. Ist die Geschichte zu Ende?*: Rowohlt.

Norris, C. (1982) *Deconstruction: Theory and Practice*, London: Methuen.

—— (1985) *The Contest of Faculties, Philosophy and Theory after Deconstruction*, London: Methuen.

—— (1987) *Jacques Derrida*, London: Fontana.

—— (1988) *Paul de Man: Deconstruction and the Critique of Aesthetic Ideology*, London: Routledge.

—— (1990) *What's Wrong with Postmodernism?*, Baltimore: Johns Hopkins University Press.

—— (1993) *The Truth About Postmodernism*, Oxford: Blackwell.

Oliva, A. B. (1982) *Transavanguardia, Intérnational*, Milan.

Pefanis, J. (1991) *Heterology and the Postmodern: Bataille, Baudrillard and Lyotard*, Durham: Duke University Press.

Peukert, D. (1989) *Max Weber's Diagnose der Moderne*, Göttingen.

Pippin, R. (1991) *Modernism as a Philosophical Problem. Dissatisfaction of European High Culture*, Oxford: Blackwell.

Portoghesi, P. (1983) *Postmodern: The Architecture of the Postindustrial Society*, New York: Rizzoli.

Putnam, H. (1981) *Realism, Truth and History*, Cambridge: Cambridge University Press.

—— (1983) *Realism and Reason*, Cambridge: Cambridge University Press.

Readings, B. (1991) *Introducing Lyotard, Art and Politics*, London: Routledge.

Reese-Schäfer, W. (1989) *Lyotard zur Einführung*, Hamburg.

Richman, M. (1982) *Reading George Bataille*, Baltimore: Johns Hopkins University Press.

Rorty, R. (1979) *Philosophy and the Mirror of Nature*, Princeton NJ: Princeton University Press.

—— (1982) *Consequences of Pragmatism*, Minneapolis: University of Minnesota Press.

—— (1989) *Contingency, Irony and Solidarity*, Cambridge: Cambridge University Press.

—— (1991a) *Essays on Heidegger and Others*, Cambridge: Cambridge University Press.

—— (1991b) *Objectivism, Relativism and Truth*, Cambridge: Cambridge University Press.

Rose, M. (1979) *Parody/Meta-fiction*, London.

—— (1991) *The Postmodern and the Postindustrial. A Critical Analysis*, Cambridge: Cambridge University Press.

Russell, C. (1985) *Poets, Prophets and Revolutionaries. The Literary Avantgarde from Rimbaud through Postmodernism*, Oxford: Oxford University Press.

Sallis, J. (ed.) (1986) *Deconstruction and Philosophy*, Chicago: Chicago University Press.

Schechner, R. (1982) *The End of Humanism. Writing on Performances*, New York.

Schulze, G. (1992) *Die Erlebnisgesellschaft. Kultursoziologie der Gegenwart*, Frankfurt/M.: Campus.

Serres, M. (1985) *Les Cinq Sens*, Paris:

Shestov, L. (1903) *Dostojevski i Nitsze. Filosofia tragedii*, St Petersburg.

—— (1939) *Athènes et Jerusalem*, Paris.

BIBLIOGRAPHY

—— (1966) *Sola fide* (Tolko wieroj), Paris.

Sloterdijk, P. (1982) *Kritik der zynischen Vernunft*, Frankfurt/M.: Suhrkamp.

—— (1987) *Kopernikanische Mobilmachung und ptolomäische Abrüstung, Aesthetischer Versuch*, Frankfurt: Suhrkamp.

Smart, B. (1992) *Modern Conditions, Postmodern Controversies*, London: Routledge.

—— (1993) *Postmodernity*, London: Routledge.

Spanos, W. (1987) *Repetitions: The Postmodern Occasions in Literature*, Baton Rouge.

Staten, H. (1984) *Wittgenstein and Derrida*, Lincoln/London: University of Nebraska Press.

Steiner, G. (1975) *Exterritorial*, Harmondsworth: Penguin.

Sukenick, R. (1969) *The Death of the Novel and Other Stories*, New York.

—— (1985) *In Form: Digressions on the Art of Fiction*, Carbondale: South Illinois University Press.

Tester, K. (1993) *The Life and Times of Postmodernity*, London: Routledge.

—— (ed.) (1994) *The Flâneur*, London: Routledge.

Torres, F. (1986) *Déjà vu. Post- et Neo-modernité*, Ramsay-Coll: Rebours.

Toulmin, S. (1972) *The Human Understanding*, Princeton NJ: Princeton University Press.

Touraine, A. (1969) *Le societé post-industrialle*, Paris: Denoël.

—— (1992) *Critique de la modernité*, Paris: Fayard.

Ulmer, G. L. (1985) *Applied Grammatology, Post(e)-Pedagogy from J. Derrida to J. Beuys*, Baltimore: Johns Hopkins University Press.

Vattimo, G. (1985a) *La fine della modernità*, Milan: Garzanti.

—— (1985b) *Al di del sogetto: Nietzsche, Heidegger et hermeneutica*, Milan.

—— (1989a) *Etica Dell'interpretatione*, Torno: Rusenberg a Séllier.

—— (1989b) *La societá transparente*, Milano: Garzanti.

Virilio, P. (1986) *Speed and Politics*, New York: Semiotext.

—— (1980) *L'esthétique de la disparition*, Paris: Galilée.

—— (1984) *L'horizon négatif*, Paris: Galilée.

—— (1990) *L'inertie polaire*, Paris: Bourgois.

Wagner, P. (1994) *A Sociology of Modernity, Liberty and Discipline*, London: Routledge.

Wallis, B. (ed.) (1984) *Art After Modernism. Rethinking Representation*, New York: New Museum of Contemporary Art.

Weber, M. (1924) *Gesammelte Aufsätze zur Sociologie u Sozialpolitik*, Tübingen: Mohr.

—— (1972) *Die protestantische Ethik und der Geist des Kapitalismus*, Tübingen: Mohr.

—— (1973) *Gesammelte Aufsätze zur Wissenschaftslehre*, Tübingen: Mohr.

Wellmer, A. (1985) *Zur Dialektik von Moderne und Postmoderne. Vernunftkritik nach Adorno*, Frankfurt: Suhrkamp.

—— (1993) *Endspiele: Die unversöhnliche Moderne*, Frankfurt: Suhrkamp.

Welsch, W. (1987a) *Aisthesis. Grundzüge und Perspektiven der Aristotelischen Sinneslehre*, Stuttgart:

—— (1987b) *Unsere postmoderne Moderne*, Weinheim VCH:

—— (1988a) (ed.) *Wege aus der Moderne – Schlüsseltexte der Postmodern – Diskussion*, Weinheim VCH:

—— (1988b) *Postmoderne als ethischer und politischer Wert*, Cologne:

—— (1990)*Aesthetisches Denken*, Stuttgart: Reclam.

—— and Pries, C. (eds) (1990) *Aesthetik im Widerstreit*, Wienheim VCH.

West, C. (1989) *The American Evasion of Philosophy. A Genealogy of Pragmatism*, Madison: University of Wisconsin Press.

White, H. (1973) *Metahistory. The Historical Imagination in Nineteenth-century Europe*, Baltimore: Johns Hopkins University Press.

—— (1978)*Topics of Discourse. Essays in Cultural Criticism*, Baltimore: Johns Hopkins University Press.

Wilde, A. (1981) *Horizons of Assent: Modernism, Postmodernism and the Ironic Imagination*, Baltimore: John Hopkins University Press.

Zimmerli, W. (ed.) (1991) *Technologisches Zeitalter oder Postmoderne?*, Munich.

Zylberberg, J. (1986) *Masses et postmodernité*, Paris: Klincksieck.

INDEX

INDEX

Warsaw: architecture 106; Church
of Our Lady of-Czestochowa
106, Plate 6a; *Gruppa* 105;
Institute of Art History and
Theory 117; postmodernism
109; Sobieski Hotel 106;
University 117–19; uprisings
117
Weber, M. 3, 6–7, 11, 23, 35, 61,
100
Welsch, W. 49, 53–6, 60, 64, 99,
111
Who Framed Roger Rabbit?
(Zemeckis) 47
Wiene, R. 2

Wienerschule 117
Wilson, R. 62
Witkiewicz, S.I. 106, 120
Wittgenstein, L. 16, 95,
117
Woźniak, P. 106

Young Frankenstein (Brooks) 36,
38–9

Z (Porebski) 108
Zanussi, K. 40
Zelig (Allen) 46
Zemeckis, R. 47
Zola, E. 28